MEDITERRANEAN DIET COOKBOOK
2022

◆··◆

150 Easy Flavorful Recipes For An
Healthier Lifestyle.
Increase Your Physical Well-Being and Keep
Your Body Weight Under Control

by Susan Lombardi

Meet The Author!

Susan Lombardi

Susan Lombardi is a cooking enthusiast who has extensively studied the most effective diets to maintain the healthiest and most balanced lifestyle possible.

She started writing recipes to spread the pleasure of eating in joy without giving up the most appetizing and delicious foods.

Her Italian origins have instilled in her a passion for food and how important it is as a means of sociability and conviviality.

Her motto is "Health comes with eating".

Table of Contents

Chapter 9: Fish And Seafood - 113

Chapter 10: Dinner - 123

Chapter 11: Snack And Appetizers - 135

Chapter 12: Desserts - 173

Chapter 13: 28 Day Mediterranean Meal Plan - 211

INTRODUCTION

The Mediterranean Diet is not just a diet but it's a way of life. This diet offers a really extended range of fresh and delicious foods from all food categories but even more. It's a different way to eat, to prepare and cook food. And we can say – no doubt - a healthier way.

The Mediterranean diet gives you the chance to enjoy many lovely dishes and even if there is more of a focus on certain food groups none are excluded.

Furthermore, this diet gives the opportunity to learn how to appreciate and prepare more fresh and seasonal food and change radically your habits. This change start including your family members. The more that are attempting this healthy lifestyle, the more likely there will be a positive outcome. Having a support system that you can depend on really comes in handy, especially when trying a radical lifestyle change.

Switch to a new diet making a lifestyle change can be tough! This book will help you step-by-step to afford this journey and will prepare you to understand this culinary tradition and all its shades and finally benefit from it lifelong.

In this book, I will be sharing with you all you need to know about the Mediterranean diet and how to get started.

Let's begin!

CHAPTER 1: WHAT IS THE MEDITERRANEAN DIET?

The Mediterranean diet is an eating pattern that follows the traditional method for eating in the nations surrounded by the Mediterranean Sea. You don't need to live in Italy, Spain or France to profit by the diet, be that as it may; numerous individuals are changing to it for the scope of health benefits it gives.

> The Mediterranean diet is not a strict plan. Or maybe, it's a method for eating that emphasizes natural products, vegetables, whole grains, vegetables and olive oil. Fish is the principle protein source rather than red meat, pork or poultry. And indeed, it remembers red wine-for balance. Aged dairy are consumed normally but in moderate sums. Eggs and poultry are occasionally expended, but red meat and prepared foods are not eaten normally.

The Mediterranean diet is associated with lower cholesterol, decreased danger of coronary illness and stroke, lower danger of Parkinson's and Alzheimer's diseases and a more drawn out life. Developing exploration shows it might also lessen danger of, and advantage those with, sadness, tension, type 2 diabetes and a few cancer growths.

If you are searching for a healthy way to lose the weight and to maintain an optimal health, then this is the best diet for you. It's the Mediterranean diet, a very popular and unique one.

The Mediterranean diet refers to the traditional eating habits and lifestyles of people living around the Mediterranean Sea – Italy, Spain, France, Greece, and some North African countries. The Mediterranean diet has become very popular in recent times, as people from these regions have better health and suffer from fewer ailments, such as cancer and cardiovascular issues. Food plays a key role in this.

Research has uncovered the many benefits of this diet. According to the results of a 2013 study, many overweight and diabetic patients showed a surprising improvement in their cardiovascular health after eating the Mediterranean diet for 5 years. The study was conducted among 7000 people in Spain. There was a marked 30% reduction in cardiovascular disease in this high-risk group.

The report took the world by storm after the New England Journal of Medicine published the findings. Several studies have indicated its many health benefits – the Mediterranean diet may stabilize the level of blood sugar, prevent Alzheimer's disease, reduce the risk of heart disease and stroke, improve brain health, ease anxiety and depression, promote weight loss, and even lower the risk of certain types of cancer.

The diet differs from country to country, and even within the regions of these countries because of cultural, ethnic, agricultural, religious, and economic differences. So there is no one standard Mediterranean diet. However, there are several common factors.

The Mediterranean Diet Food Pyramid

The Med diet food pyramid is a nutrition guide to help people eat the right foods in the correct quantities and the prescribed frequency as per the traditional eating habits of people from the Mediterranean coast countries.

The pyramid was developed by the World Health Organization, Harvard School of Public Health, and the old ways Preservation Trust in 1993.

The Med diet food pyramid is a nutrition guide to help people eat the right foods in the correct quantities and the prescribed frequency as per the traditional eating habits of people from the Mediterranean coast countries.

The pyramid was developed by the World Health Organization, Harvard School of Public Health, and the old ways Preservation Trust in 1993.

There are 6 food layers in the pyramid with physical activity at the base, which is an important element to maintain a healthy life.

Just above it is the first food layer, consisting of whole grains, breads, beans, pasta, and nuts. It is the strongest layer having foods that are recommended by the Mediterranean diet. Next comes fruits and vegetables. As you move up the pyramid, you will find foods that must be eaten less and less, with the topmost layer consisting of foods that should be avoided or restricted.

The Mediterranean diet food pyramid is easy to understand. It provides an easy way to follow the eating plan.

The Food Layers: *Whole Grains, Breads, Beans* – The lowest and the widest layer with foods that are strongly recommended. Your meals should be made of mostly these items. Eat whole-wheat bread, whole-wheat pita, whole-grain roll and bun, whole-grain cereal, whole-wheat pasta, and brown rice. 4 to 6 servings a day will give you plenty of nutrition.

Olive oil – Cook your meals preferably in extra-virgin olive oil. Daily consumption. Healthy for the body, it lowers the low-density lipoprotein cholesterol (LDL) and total cholesterol level. Up to 2 tablespoons of olive oil is allowed. The diet also allows canola oil..

Fruits, Vegetables – Almost as important as the lowest layer. Eat non-starchy vegetables daily like asparagus, broccoli, beets, tomatoes, carrots, cucumber, cabbage, cauliflower, turnips 4 to 8 servings daily. Take 2 to 4 servings of fruits every day.
Choose seasonal fresh fruits.

Poultry, cheese, yogurt – The diet should include cheese, yogurt, eggs, chicken, and other poultry products, but in moderation. Maximum 2-3 times in a week. Low-fat dairy is best.
Soy milk, cheese, or yogurt is better.

Meats, sweets – This is the topmost layer consisting of foods that are best avoided. Red meats you can have them once or twice in a weekly max, sweets only one time at month. Remember, the Mediterranean diet is plant-based. There is very little room for meat, especially red meat. If you cannot live without it, then take red meat in small portions. Choose lean cuts. Have sweets only to celebrate. For instance, you can have a couple of sweets after following the diet for a month.

◆ Recommended Foods ◆

For example, most people living in the region eat a diet rich in whole grains, vegetables, fruits, nuts, seeds, fish, fats, and legumes. It is not a restrictive diet like the many low-fat eating plans. Actually, fat is encouraged, but only from healthy sources, such as polyunsaturated fat (omega-3 fatty acids) that you will get from fish and monounsaturated fat from olive oil.

It is strongly plant-based, but not exclusively vegetarian. The diet recommends limiting the intake of saturated fats and trans fats that you get from red meat and processed foods. You must also limit the intake of dairy products.

Fruits and vegetables – Eat daily. Try to have 7-10 servings every day. Meals are strongly based on plant-based foods. Eat fresh fruits and vegetables. Pick from seasonal varieties.

Whole grains – Eat whole-grain cereal, bread, and pasta. All parts of whole grains – the germ, bran, and the endosperm provide healthy nutrients. These nutrients are lost when the grain is refined into white flour.

Healthy fats only – Avoid butter for cooking. Switch to olive oil. Dip your bread in flavored olive oil instead of applying margarine or butter on bread. Trans fats and saturated fats can cause heart disease.

Fish – Fish is encouraged. Eat fatty fish like herring, mackerel, albacore tuna, sardines, lake trout, and salmon. Fatty fish will give you plenty of healthy omega-3 fatty acids that reduce inflammations. Omega-3 fatty acids also reduced blood clotting, decreased triglycerides, and improves heart health. Eat fresh seafood two times a week. Avoid deep-fried fish. Choose grilled fish.

Legumes – Provides the body with minerals, protein, complex carbohydrates, polyunsaturated fatty acids, and fiber. Eat daily.

Dairy and poultry – You can eat eggs, milk products, and chicken throughout the week, but with moderation. Restrict cheese.
Go for plain or low-fat Greek yogurt instead of cheese.

Nuts and seeds – 3 or more servings every week. Eat a variety of nuts, seeds, and beans. Walnuts and almonds are all allowed.

Red meat – The Mediterranean diet is not meat-based. You can still have red meat, but only once or twice a week max. If you love red meat, then make sure that it is lean. Take small portions only. Avoid processed meats like salami, sausage, and bologna.

Olive Oil – The key source of fat. Olive oil will give you monounsaturated fat that lowers the LDL or low-density lipoprotein cholesterol and total cholesterol level. Seeds and nuts will also provide you monounsaturated fat. You can also have canola oil but no cream, butter, mayonnaise, or margarine. Take up to 4 tablespoons of olive oil a day. For best results, only take extra-virgin olive oil.

Wine – Red wine is allowed, but with moderation. Don't take more than a glass of red wine daily. Best take only 3-4 days a week.

Desserts – Say no to ice cream, sweets, pies, and chocolate cake. It's better to replace sweets with fresh fruits.

Main Components:

1. *Focus on natural foods* – Avoid processed foods as much as you can;
2. *Be flexible* – Plan to have a variety of foods;
3. Consume fruits, vegetables, healthy fats, and whole grains daily;
4. Have weekly plans for poultry, fish, eggs, and beans;
5. Take dairy products moderately;
6. Limit red meat intake;
7. Take water instead of soda. Only take wine when you are having a meal.

The Med Lifestyle

Not just the food, but the correct lifestyle is also equally important. This includes both getting adequate exercise and making social connections.

Physical Activity – It is at the base of the food pyramid, even lower than the first and most important food layer – getting adequate physical activity is essential. This includes exercising regularly, swimming, biking, running, and playing an active sport. However, there are other ways as well to maintain good health.

You will find many from the Mediterranean region not going to the gym. But, they are not inactive. Many are into a lot of manual labor. They will walk to their workplace, to the bakery, or the farmer's market. They walk to their friend's home. Even a daily walk and moderate exercise will help. Natural movements are good. Avoid the escalator. Take the stairs instead.

How much exercising is good? Working out is always good for health. You don't have to lift weights, though. 10-15 minutes on the treadmill and gym bike 5 days a week should be good. Half an hour of moderate-intensity activity will do. Nothing better if you can also do a few muscle-strengthening activities twice a week. You can also try walking 200 minutes a week or even gardening for an hour 4-5 times a week.

Cook at Home – Home cooked food is always healthier than eating out. For example, restaurant cooked pasta will have higher portions of sodium. Again, you can have one portion of whole-grain spaghetti with tomato sauce and spinach instead of the heavy cream sauce. You can control the ingredients by preparing the meals at home. Home cooked meals have lots of minerals, vitamins, and fiber, and are lower in added sugar, sodium, and saturated fat.

Eat Together – The mealtime should be a social experience. Eating together with friends or family is a great source of energy and helps reduce stress. It will boost your mood, which will have a positive impact on your physical health. Plus, it will prevent you from overeating too. You will often find the Mediterranean people eating together in a garden.

Switch the TV off and enjoy your meal. Monitor what the kids are eating. If you live alone, invite a co-worker, neighbor, or friend. You can even invite someone and prepare meals together.

Laugh Often – Have you heard of the popular saying, "Laughter is the best medicine"? This is true in the Mediterranean culture. Many are individuals with a big personality. Their conversations are full of humor. They love to tell stories. Enjoy life and keep a positive attitude.

Live a Simple Life – Consider food, for example. You won't find them buying too much of anything. The idea of buying any ingredient in bulk is foreign to them. They buy fresh, focusing on daily needs. And of course, fresh food is always best.

Enjoy Every Bite – Slow down and enjoy each bite. Many will eat for survival. But in the Mediterranean belt, they love their food. They enjoy it. Don't eat on the go. Sit down and

CHAPTER 2: BENEFITS OF THE MEDITERRANEAN DIET

> *Heart disease and stroke* – The Mediterranean diet recommends limited eating of processed foods, red meat, and refined breads, which contributes towards a lower risk of heart ailments and stroke. A study carried out over 12 years among 25,000 women found that women eating this diet were able to reduce their risk of heart disease by 25%.

The **PREDIMED** study was carried out amongst men and women with a high-risk of cardiovascular disease and type-2 diabetes in Spain. After 5 years of research, it was discovered that those who had a calorie-unrestricted Mediterranean diet had a 30% lower risk of heart issues.

> *Alzheimer's* – Research also suggests that the diet can improve blood sugar levels, cholesterol, and blood vessel health, which in turn may lower the risk of dementia and Alzheimer's disease. A 2018 study (scanned the brains of 70 people for dementia and monitored their food habits. After 2 years, it was observed that those on the Mediterranean diet had fewer protein plaques or beta-amyloid deposits than others, and thus a lower risk of Alzheimer's.

Other studies have also revealed that the Mediterranean diet may also prevent the decline of thinking skills and memory with age as there is an increased supply of oxygen and nutrients to the brain.

The diet is packed with antioxidants, such as olive oil and nuts, which may delay mental decline. A link between consuming fish and lower risk of Alzheimer's has also been found.

> *Diabetes* – The diet with healthy carbs and whole grains offers big benefits like stabilizing the blood sugar level. Complex whole grain carbs like wheat berries, buckwheat, and quinoa improves overall energy and keeps the sugar level even in your blood. Research on more than 400 people between the age of 55 and 80 years have revealed that the Mediterranean diet can lower (the risk of type-2 diabetes by 52%. This study was carried out over 4 years.

Parkinson's disease – The diet is rich in antioxidants, which may prevent oxidative stress or cell damage, thus reducing the risk of Parkinson's disease by as much as 50%.

Weight loss – The Mediterranean diet gives you plenty of fiber that will make you feel satiated. You won't overeat as a result. The diet improves metabolism and promotes healthy weight loss. Just remember to focus on consuming fibrous vegetables, fruits, beans, and legumes instead of simple carbohydrates. This is a safe and sustainable way to lose weight as almost nothing is denied in the overall meal plan. The U.S. News & World Report ranked Mediterranean diet #1 in the 'Best Overall Diet' category for 2019.

Cancer – The diet has also been linked to a lower risk of certain types of cancer. Researchers looked at the findings of 83 studies covering more than 2 million people and concluded that it may reduce (the risk of breast, gastric, colorectal, and colon cancer. The cancer mortality rate is significantly lower amongst those who eat this diet. This has been attributed to the higher intake of whole grains, vegetables, and fruits. The result of this study was published in the Nutrients journal.

Another study according to the JAMA Internal Medicine journal discovered that women eating this diet were able to reduce the risk of breast cancer by 62%.

Inflammation – Fatty fish like tuna, mackerel, and salmon have a lot of omega-3 fatty acids that can reduce inflammation. Besides, the omega-3 will also improve the elasticity of your skin and make it stronger.

Rheumatoid arthritis – In this autoimmune disease, the body's immune system attacks the joints by mistake, causing swelling and pain. The National Institutes of Health's Office of Dietary Supplements has suggested that long-chain omega-3 fatty acids, which you will find in fatty fish provides relief from the symptoms of RA or Rheumatoid arthritis.

Good for the gut – The Med diet provides 7% more good bacteria in the microbiome, compared to those eating a traditional western diet as it is a plant-based eating plan with a lot of fruits, vegetables, nuts, seeds, and legumes. This improves gut health.

Several other scientific studies have also revealed the health gains of eating this diet.

The Rockefeller Foundation – This was one of the first studies on the diet carried out on the Greek island of Crete. The Greek government asked for help from the Rockefeller Foundation after the World War II because the island was severely destructed after the war and the people were in abject poverty. Many field staff were sent, including nutritionists and nurses.

They visited many homes and took notes on their food and drinking habits. To their surprise, it was found that most people were of good health and were living into old age in spite of the poverty. Very few people were suffering from heart disease, though 40% of their calories were coming from fat.

Ancel Keys' 7 Country Study – This was a follow-up study to find out the heart health condition of residents around the Mediterranean Sea. It was carried out in the late 1950s by Ancel Keys, the American scientist. In the late 1950s, 92 out of 1000 men in the United States were suffering from heart diseases. But in Crete, Ancel found to his surprise, that only 3 men out of 1000 had heart conditions.

The University of Barcelona Study – In recent time, the University of Barcelona Carried out a study on 7000 men and women over 5 years. They found that there were significant improvements in heart health when the participants ate a Mediterranean diet. The risk of cardiovascular disease dropped by almost 30%. And they were also high-risk individuals, as the participants were all overweight people, and also diabetics and smokers. The results of this 2013 study was published by the New England Journal of Medicine.

The Cochrane Study – Carried out in the same year, this study too arrived at the same conclusion. The researchers concluded by noting that a high-protein, high-fiber, low-glycemic index, low-carbohydrate diet improves cardiovascular health and reduces the risk of diabetes.

Hundreds of studies have been carried out in recent years to verify whether the diet improves health or not. Almost all of them have concluded that those who eat a Mediterranean diet have lower risks of Alzheimer's, dementia, and diabetes. Many other health advantages have also been noted.

Chapter 3: What Foods Can I Eat on This Diet?

The heft of your diet ought to incorporate regular, natural Mediterranean foods. This diet is extremely unrestrictive, and you'll have the option to appreciate a lot of delectable foods. You may even find some new top choices!

You should go for a wide assortment of foods, to guarantee that you're getting an equalization of supplements, nutrients, and minerals. Whole, single fixing foods are basic for benefiting as much as possible from your Mediterranean lifestyle.

Concentrate on eating these foods

1. *Tubers*: These dull vegetables ought to be expended with some restraint, but are as yet a significant piece of this diet. Appreciate potatoes, sweet potatoes, turnips, and yams.

2. *Whole grains*: Avoid refined sugars, but eat small servings of things like whole oats, darker rice, rye, grain, corn, buckwheat, whole wheat, and whole grains.

3. *Poultry*: Occasionally, appreciate chicken, duck, turkey, or different winged animals.

4. *Healthy fats*: This is a significant piece of the Mediterranean diet, so ensure you're getting a lot of fats from olive oil, nuts, and avocado.

Note that anybody with issues with alcohol use ought to abstain from consuming wine, despite the fact that it is energized with this diet.

Avoid these Unhealthy Foods

You ought to maintain a strategic distance from these unhealthy foods and ingredients:

1. **Added sugar**: Soda, candies, frozen yogurt, table sugar and numerous others.
2. **Tran's fats**: Found in margarine and different handled foods.
3. **Processed meat**: Processed hotdogs, franks, and so on.
4. **Highly handled foods**: Anything marked "low-fat" or "diet" or which seems as though it was made in a manufacturing plant.

You should peruse food names cautiously if you want to dodge these unhealthy ingredients.

What to Drink

1. Water ought to be your go-to drink on a Mediterranean diet.
2. This diet also incorporates moderate measures of *red wine* — around 1 glass for every day.
3. Nonetheless, this is totally discretionary, and wine ought to be maintained a strategic distance from by anybody with liquor abuse or issues controlling their use.
4. Espresso and tea are also totally adequate, but you ought to keep away from sugar-improved refreshments and natural product juices, which are exceptionally high in sugar.

Chapter 4: How to Follow the Mediterranean Diet. Tips and Tricks

1. **Plan your meals** – Plan your meals in advance. Plan what you want to eat throughout the week when you have time during the weekend. This includes the snacks too. Then make sure that you have the necessary ingredients in advance. It will be easier for you to eat healthy throughout the week. You can even prepare a few meals in advance, especially those you can refrigerate.

2. **Cook with olive oil** – Don't use coconut oil or vegetable oil. Extra-virgin olive oil is strongly recommended. Olive oil provides monounsaturated fatty acids that will improve your HDL cholesterol level (the good type). A 2017 study even shows that HDL cholesterol can remove LDL particles from the arteries. Drizzle some olive oil on your food to improve flavor.

3. **Meat-free days** – The Med diet is mostly plant-based with some fish. Pulses, beans, and fish will give you all the proteins you need. Meat is only allowed once or twice a weekly. Chicken is better than red meat.

4. **Adopt** – Mediterranean flavors might not go precisely with all cuisines. However, you can still adopt many elements. For instance, while preparing something spicy like curry, you can use oils with unsaturated fats. Olive oil is the best. Sunflower and rapeseed oil is better than palm oil or coconut oil.

5. **Antioxidants** – Eat vegetables and fruits packed with antioxidants. This will give you pterostilbene, resveratrol, and glutathione. You will get glutathione from onions, garlic, cruciferous vegetables, and spinach. Raspberries and blueberries will provide resveratrol. Oregano, mint, basil and such other herbs will give you other key antioxidants for good health.

6. **Eat wholesome** – Pasta, an Italian favorite from the Mediterranean region, also fits into the plan. Prioritize whole-grain options, but you will find grain-free options as well to eliminate having more grains.

7. **Snacking** – Have nuts for snacks. Keep a handful of cashews, pistachios, or almonds with you. They are all very satisfying. The Nutrition Journal published a study where it was found that those who replaced chips, cookies, cereal bars, and crackers with almonds ended up adding fewer empty calories, sodium, and added sugar. Nuts will also provide you with essential minerals and fiber.

Once you've started and are fully immersed in the Mediterranean diet, you might notice that you've started to feel a little bit weak, and a little bit colder, than you're used to. The Mediterranean diet places an emphasis on trying to cut out as much sodium from your diet as possible, which is very healthy for some of us who already have high sodium levels. Sodium, obviously is found in salt, and so we proceed to cut out salt – and then drink enough water to drain every last drop of sodium from our bodies. When it comes to hydration, the biological mechanisms for keeping us saturated and quenched rely on an equal balance of sodium and potassium. Sodium can be found in your interstitial fluid, and potassium can be found inside our cytoplasm – two sides of one wall. When you drink tons of water, sweat a lot at the gym, or both, your sodium leaves your body in your urine and your sweat. Potassium, on the other hand, is only really lost through the urine – and even then, it's rare. This means that our bodies almost constantly need a refill on our sodium levels. But if you aren't eating any salt, or drinking any salt, then where are you supposed to get the salt that will help you stay hydrated? Plenty of individuals on the Mediterranean diet choose to manage their hydration through pills, instead of simply adding more salt back into their foods. This is actually a smart route, because sodium taken orally will make it to your blood stream faster.

If you haven't heard of the term "meal prep" before now, it's a beautiful day to learn something that will save you time, stress, and inches on your waistline. Meal prep, short for meal preparation, is a habit that was developed mostly by the body building community in order to accurately track your macronutrients. You will get to go further in-depth about tracking your macronutrients in the next section, but meal prep is one of the most convenient ways to do so. If you work a nine to five job like most of us, you know the struggle of feeding yourself a healthy dinner after work when you're tired, hungry, and just want to go home. When western society started getting more and more fast paced, we developed the fast food restaurant that could serve you from your car. While we all love to indulge in a little junk food now and then, fast food restaurants are marketed more towards routine family use than to a one-off indulgence. If you have kids, you're probably even more familiar with this struggle. Some of the members of the fitness community had finally had enough, and so they developed a way to cook healthy, homemade meals every single week without busting the bank, sacrificing time in the gym, or sacrificing time with your loved ones. The basic idea behind meal prep is that each weekend, you manage your free time around cooking and preparing all of your meals for the upcoming week. While most meal preppers do their grocery shopping and cooking on Sundays, to keep their meals the most fresh, you can choose to cook on a Saturday if that works better with your schedule. Meal prep each week uses one large grocery list of bulk ingredients to get all the supplies you need to make four dinners and four lunches of your choice. This means that you might have to a bit of mental math quadrupling the serving size, but all you have to do is multiply each ingredient by four. Although you don't have to meal prep more than one meal with four portions each week, if you're already in the kitchen, you most likely have cooking time to work on something else. Many body builders even prep their breakfasts and on-the-go snacks during the weekend, to save time and make absolutely sure they know what they're eating. For the average person, meal prepping four dinners alone will already free up a ton of time during the week – for a gym session, perhaps, or more time relaxing with the family. When you cook for meal prep, you're going to be creating one meal in four portions – which can take up a lot of dishes. Investing in some good pots, pans, and skillets will help you work more efficiently in the kitchen, and matching Tupperware are something a good meal prepper can never resist. Once you've cooked your entire four-portion meal in one batch, you can separate out individual matching portions that you will eat throughout the week.

Most cooked vegetables and meats can last for up to five days in the refrigerator, but you can feel free to freeze your entrees as well if you need the space. Vegetables that are uncooked normally have three to four days only, but that's why you're only reaching about four days in advance. If you want to keep your meals fresher for longer, you can always look for glass Tupperware with locking seals that can keep freshness in for longer. Each week, you can do repeat this process with new recipes and new ingredients. However, it's worth it to note that if you're someone who likes consistency, meal prepping might be a bit of an adjustment. Meal prep tends to make only one identical dinner meal and one identical lunch meal each week – which means that eaters who like to have a different dinner each night might have their work cut out for them. One of the easiest ways to combat this is by simply making a dinner and a lunch that can be interchanged whenever necessary to create variety. Once you've learned how to meal prep, you will save yourself enough time in the evenings relax, practice some self-care, and really extend your dinner hours to have fun conversation with friends and family. Now, meal preparation isn't just a cool technique to save you time and money – meal prep at its very core was designed to help you manage your weight loss in a convenient way, which is exactly what you need to succeed.

Tracking Your Macronutrients

Wouldn't it be nice if you could have a full nutritional label for each of your home-cooked meals, just to make sure that your numbers are adding up in favor of weight loss? Oddly enough, tracking your macronutrients in order to calculate the nutritional value of each of your meals and portions is as easy as stepping on the scale. Not the scale in your bathroom, however. A food scale! If you've never had a good relationship with your weight and numbers, you might suddenly find that they aren't too bad after all. Food scales are used to measure, well, your food, but there's a slick system of online calculators and fitness applications for you smart phone that can take this number and turn it into magic. When you meal prep each week, keep track of your recipes diligently. Remember how you multiplied each of the ingredients on the list by four to create four servings? You're going to want to remember how much of each vegetable, fruit, grain, nut, and fat you cooked with. While you wait for you meal to finish cooking, find a large enough plastic container to fit all of your meal.

Make sure it's clean and dry, and use the empty container to zero out your scale. Once you've finished cooking your entire meal, transfer *all four portions* into the clean plastic container and take not of the weight. When you use your online calculator or fitness app, you can enter the amount of each ingredient you used to cook the meal, and then the weight of the entire four portions. This will give you an estimate of how many carbohydrates, proteins, and fats are contained within each dish, and how many overall calories your meal comes out to be. Now, you're obviously not going to be consuming all of this at once, and so you will have to divide each number by four in order to get the proper readings. At the end of this process, you will have an almost entirely complete nutritional label for a meal that you made at home, from fresh and healthy ingredients that you know won't make you gain weight. It's one of the many ways that the Mediterranean diet turns something tedious like math and intimidating like scales into a delicious and nutritious way of living a healthier, and happier, life. Speaking of scales, let's talk a little bit about using the caloric estimates on your homemade meals to track your calories, and implicate a deficit, in order to lose more weight than you ever thought possible.

Goal Setting to Meet Your Achievements

On the subject of control, there are a few steps and activities that you should go through before you begin your Mediterranean diet just to make sure that you have clear and realistic goals in mind. Sitting down to set goals before embarking on a totally new diet routine will help you stay focused and committed during your Mediterranean diet. While a Mediterranean diet lifestyle certainly isn't as demanding as some of the crazy diet fads you see today, it can be a struggle to focus on eating natural fruits and vegetables that are more "salt of the Earth" foods than we're used to. You already know that when it comes to weight loss, you shouldn't expect to lose more than one to two pounds per week healthily while you're dieting. You are still welcome to set a weight loss goal with time in mind, but when it comes to the Mediterranean diet, you should set your goals for one month in the future. One month might seem like a long time, but for a diet that's designed to be integrated into your lifestyle, one month will give you a great concept of what you can expect in the year to come. When you set your goals, you should take the time to write down two lists of three bullet points for each goal. The first set should be the three most important reasons to you that you've decided to commit to the Mediterranean diet.

The second three should be three helpful tips you have for yourself or ways you can imagine reaching your goal. When you find yourself struggling on days where hunger pangs come more often than usual or the gym didn't go very well, you can look back at your two lists to remind yourself of why you're here in the first place, and the solutions that past you knew future you could handle. Dieting is difficult for all of us, but taking the time to care for yourself and your mental state on a diet can have a huge impact on your happiness (and on your weight loss). One of the next goals you should set for your personal journey on the Mediterranean diet is a meal prepping goal. You're going to be surprised at how easy meal prepping actually is, but a lot of the time you can fall victim to your own laziness after a while. To encourage yourself to continue meal prepping, you should set certain goals each week about new snacks you can prepare.

Cooking multiple dinner meals in one weekend, or trying to meal prep for a dinner party. The more you challenge yourself to learn, the easier your Mediterranean diet will become over time. Nobody likes to get bored, but if you start to slack off with your cooking, you will definitely notice it in your waistline. One of the coolest thing about meal prep is that you'll start to pick up cooking techniques, knife skills, and an intuition about seasonings that you might never have thought possible. Each one of these skills will help speed up your meal prepping process, and, you'll be that much more likely to impress your friends with you skills in the kitchen. The final goal that you should set with yourself as you embark on your Mediterranean diet journey is to be kind to yourself.

While this might seem silly, you know the effect that stress can have on your body – and it simply isn't worth it to get worked up and anxious about your weight loss goals. Before you being your diet, promise yourself that you will be gentle, patient, and supportive when you need help – and yet also push yourself when you feel like you aren't progressing quickly enough. Sometimes, we have to be our own coaches, and you shouldn't be afraid to tell yourself the hard truth every now and then. With this nutritional guide at your back, there's no excuse for anything but success if you have the right drive and level of commitment. Now that you've set down come concrete goals that are going to move you forward, you deserve a bit of a treat. Quite literally, let's get into the delicious details of some thirty-minute homemade Mediterranean diet recipes.

CHAPTER 5: BREAKFAST

Breakfast Egg on Avocado

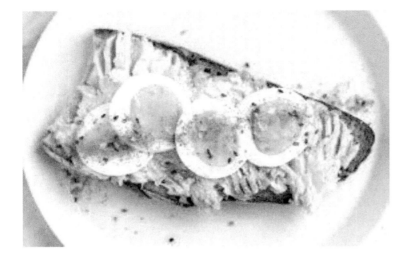

Servings: 6

Preparation Time: 10 minutes

Cooking Time: 15 minutes

Ingredients:

- 1 tsp of garlic powder
- ½ tsp of sea salt
- ¼ cup of Parmesan cheese (grated or shredded)
- 1/4 tsp of black pepper
- 3 medium avocados (cut in half, pitted, skin on)
- 6 medium eggs

Directions:

1. Prepare muffin tins and preheat the oven to 350° F.
2. To ensure that the egg would fit inside the cavity of the avocado, lightly scrape off 1/3 of the meat.
3. Place avocado on muffin tin to ensure that it faces with the top up.
4. Evenly season each avocado with pepper, salt, and garlic powder.
5. Add one egg on each avocado cavity and garnish tops with cheese.
6. Pop in the oven and bake until the egg white is set, about 15 minutes.

Nutritional Values Per Serving

Calories	Protein	Carbs	Fat
252	12 g	4 g	20 g

Breakfast Egg-artichoke Casserole

Servings: 8

Preparation Time: 10 minutes

Cooking Time: 35 minutes

Ingredients:

- 16 large eggs
- 14 oz of can artichoke hearts, drained
- 10 oz of box frozen chopped spinach, thawed and drained well
- 1 cup of shredded white cheddar
- 1 garlic clove, minced
- 1 tsp of salt
- ½ cup of parmesan cheese
- ½ cup of ricotta cheese
- ½ tsp of dried thyme
- ½ tsp of crushed red pepper
- ¼ cup of milk
- ¼ cup of shaved onion

Directions:

1. Lightly grease a 9x13 inch baking dish with cooking spray and preheat the oven to 350° F.
2. In a large mixing bowl, add eggs and milk. Mix thoroughly.
3. With a paper towel, squeeze out the excess moisture from the spinach leaves and add to the bowl of eggs. Into small pieces, break the artichoke hearts and separate the leaves. Add to the bowl of eggs.
4. Except for the ricotta cheese, add remaining ingredients in the bowl of eggs and mix thoroughly.
5. Pour egg mixture into the prepared dish.
6. Evenly add dollops of ricotta cheese on top of the eggs and then pop in the oven.
7. Bake until eggs are set and doesn't jiggle when shook, about 35 minutes.
8. Remove from the oven and evenly divide into suggested servings.

Calories	Protein	Carbs	Fat
302	22.6 g	10.8 g	18.7 g

Brekky Egg-potato Hash

Servings: 2

Preparation Time: 10 minutes

Cooking Time: 25 minutes

Ingredients:

o 1 zucchini, diced

o ½ cup of chicken broth

o ½ pound of cooked chicken

o 1 tbsp of olive oil

o 4 oz of shrimp

o salt and ground black pepper to taste

o 1 large sweet potato, diced

o 2 eggs

o ¼ tsp of cayenne pepper

o 2 tsp of garlic powder

o *1 cup of fresh spinach (optional)*

Directions:

1. In a skillet, add the olive oil.
2. Fry the shrimp, cooked chicken and sweet potato for 2 minutes.
3. Add the cayenne pepper, garlic powder and salt, and toss for 4 minutes.
4. Add the zucchini and toss for another 3 minutes.
5. Whisk the eggs in a bowl and add to the skillet.
6. Season using salt and pepper. Cover with the lid.
7. Cook for 1 minute and add the chicken broth.
8. Cover and cook for another 8 minutes on high heat.
9. Add the spinach and toss for 2 more minutes.

Nutritional Values Per Serving

Calories	Protein	Carbs	Fat
190	11.7 g	2.9 g	12.3 g

Dill and Tomato Frittata

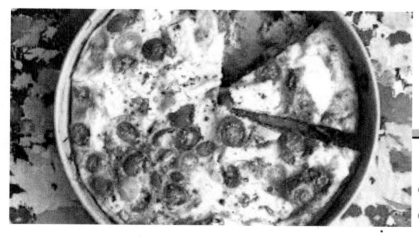

Servings: 6

Preparation Time: 10 minutes

Cooking Time: 35 minutes

Ingredients:

- pepper and salt to taste
- 1 tsp of red pepper flakes
- 2 garlic cloves, minced
- ½ cup of crumbled goat cheese (optional)
- 2 tbsp of fresh chives, chopped
- 2 tbsp of fresh dill, chopped
- 4 tomatoes, diced
- 8 eggs, whisked
- 1 tsp of coconut oil

Directions:

1. Grease a 9 inch round baking pan and preheat oven to 325° F.
2. In a large bowl, mix well all ingredients and pour into prepped pan.
3. Pop into the oven and bake until middle is cooked through around 30-35 minutes.
4. Remove from oven and garnish with more chives and dill.

Nutritional Values Per Serving

Calories	Protein	Carbs	Fat
149	13.26 g	9.93 g	10.28 g

Servings: 2

Preparation Time: 10 minutes

Cooking Time: 25 minutes

Ingredients:

- 2 tsp of butter
- salt and pepper to taste
- 2 whole grain seeded ciabatta rolls, split, toasted
- 2 slices of Swiss cheese or Muenster cheese
- ½ cup of egg whites, beaten
- 2 tsp minced fresh herbs of your choice
- 2 tbsp of pesto

For roasted tomatoes:

- 2 tbsp of extra-virgin olive oil
- 20 oz of grape tomatoes, halved lengthwise
- kosher salt to taste
- coarsely ground pepper to taste

Directions:

1. Heat a nonstick pan over medium flame.
2. Toss half the butter and once it starts melting, add half the egg whites.
3. Sprinkle salt, pepper, and 1 teaspoon of herbs, and cook until the omelet is set. Flip sides and cook the other side for about 30 seconds. Place onto a plate.
4. Repeat the first steps and make the other omelet.
5. Meanwhile make the roasted tomatoes as follows: Add tomatoes into a baking dish. Pour oil over it and toss well. Sprinkle with salt and pepper. Spread it evenly in the dish.
6. Roast in a preheated oven at 400° F for about 20 minutes or charred slightly.
7. Toast the rolls just before serving.
8. Spread pesto on the cut part of the rolls.
9. Place bottom halves of the rolls on individual serving plates. Place an omelet (fold the omelet to fit in) on each.
10. Place a slice of cheese on each. Cover with top half of the rolls and serve.

Calories	Protein	Carbs	Fat	Fiber
458	21 g	51 g	24 g	2 g

Mediterranean Breakfast Casserole

Servings: 3

Preparation Time: 10 minutes

Cooking Time: 35 minutes

Ingredients:

- 1 tbsp of olive oil
- 1 medium potato, peeled, diced
- ½ pound of zucchini, sliced
- 1 small onion, chopped
- 2 medium sweet peppers, roasted, peeled
- 2 Portobello mushroom caps, chopped
- 1 cup chopped fresh spinach
- 3.5 oz of light ricotta cheese
- 3.5 oz of ricotta cheese
- 3 tbsp of part-skim milk mozzarella cheese, grated
- 2 tbsp of Pecorino Romano cheese, grated
- 6 grape tomatoes, sliced into thirds
- 1 cup of egg whites
- 1 sourdough roll, cubed

Directions:

1. Place onion and potato in a baking dish. Drizzle a teaspoon of oil over it. Toss well and tilt the dish so it spreads evenly.
2. Bake in a preheated oven at 400° F for about 15 minutes. Transfer on to a baking tray.
3. Add zucchini into a bowl. Drizzle a teaspoon of oil over it. Toss well and transfer on to the baking tray (with potatoes). Bake for another 40 minutes or until golden brown.
4. Place a skillet over medium heat. Add 1 teaspoon oil. Once the oil heats, add mushrooms and sauté until soft. Remove from the pan and set aside.

5. Add zucchini, onion potato mixture, onion, sour dough roll cubes, and grape tomatoes into a baking dish and mix well.

6. Pour the ricotta mixture over it. Sprinkle mozzarella cheese and Pecorino Romano cheese.

7. Bake in a preheated oven at 400° F for 40-50 minutes or until the eggs are cooked as per your desire. Remove the baking dish from the oven and let it cool down for a couple of minutes. Cut it into slices and serve.

8. Add 1 teaspoon oil to the same pan and place the pan over heat. Add spinach and cook well, and then turn off the heat when the spinach wilts.

9. Add ricotta cheese and egg whites into a bowl and whisk well. Set aside.

Nutritional Values Per Serving

Calories	Protein	Carbs	Fat	Fiber
370.2	25.8 g	34.4 g	15.7 g	4.6 g

Servings: 4

Preparation Time: 10 minutes

Cooking Time: 35 minutes

Ingredients:

o 3 small ripe bananas, mashed

o 2 tbsp of pure maple syrup

o 1 tsp of raw vanilla extract

o ½ tsp of ground cloves

o ¼ tsp of salt or pepper to taste

o 1 ¼ cups of unsweetened vanilla almond milk

o ¼ tsp of ground allspice

o 2 tbsp of molasses

o ½ tsp of ground ginger

o ½ tbsp of ground cinnamon

o ½ cup of quinoa, uncooked

o 2 tbsp of slivered almonds

Directions:

1. Add banana, maple syrup, vanilla, ginger, molasses, salt and all the spices into a casserole dish or baking dish. Mix until well incorporated.

2. Stir in the quinoa.

3. Add milk and whisk until well incorporated. Cover and chill overnight.

4. Remove the dish from the refrigerator and give it a good stir. Cover the dish with foil.

5. Bake in a preheated oven at 400° F for 40-50 minutes or until dry and cooked through.

6. Set the oven to broil mode. Scatter the almonds on top. Press lightly to adhere.

7. Broil for three to four minutes or until almonds are golden brown on top.

8. Remove the baking dish from the oven and let it cool for five to eight minutes. Cut it into four equal wedges and serve.

Calories	Protein	Carbs	Fat	Fiber
213	5 g	41 g	4 g	4 g

Egg Muffins with Vegetables and Feta Cheese

Servings: 6

Preparation Time: 10 minutes

Cooking Time: 15 minutes

Ingredients:

o 1 cup of finely chopped baby spinach

o ½ cup of chopped tomatoes

o ½ tbsp of chopped fresh oregano

o 4 eggs, well beaten

o ½ cup of crumbled feta cheese

o ¼ cup of finely chopped onions

o ¼ cup of chopped, pitted Kalamata olives

o 1 tsp of sunflower oil + extra to grease

o ½ cup of cooked quinoa

Directions:

1. Grease a 6 counts muffin tin with some oil.

2. Heat a skillet over medium flame and add oil. Add onions and cook until they turn translucent.

3. Grease a 6 counts muffin tin with some oil.

4. Heat a skillet over medium flame and add oil. Add onions and cook until they turn translucent.

5. Stir in the tomatoes and cook for a minute. Stir in the spinach and cook until it wilts.

6. Remove from heat.

7. Add olives and oregano and mix well.

8. Add quinoa, salt, and feta cheese into the bowl of beaten eggs and whisk well.

9. Add the sautéed vegetables and mix well.

10. Spoon into prepared muffin tins.

11. Bake in a preheated oven at 350° F for about 25 – 30 minutes or until it is done and the top is light golden brown.

12. Remove from the oven and cool for a few minutes.

13. Run a knife around the edges of the muffin and loosen the muffins. Invert onto a plate and serve.

Nutritional Values Per Serving

Calories	Protein	Carbs	Fat	Fiber
114	7 g	6 g	7 g	1 g

◆ Mediterranean Breakfast Stir Fry (Melamen) ◆

Servings: 8

Preparation Time: 10 minutes

Cooking Time: 15 minutes

Ingredients:

o 3 cups of chopped onions

o 3 cups of green bell peppers, chopped

o 4 large tomatoes, chopped

o 2 tbsp of extra-virgin olive oil

o 2 eggs, beaten

o pepper to taste

o salt to taste

Directions:

1. Heat a pan over a high flame. Add oil and then add bell pepper and sauté for a couple of minutes.

2. Reduce heat, cover and cook for two minutes.

3. Add onions and stir. Cover and cook for four to five minutes.

4. Add tomatoes, salt and pepper, stir and cover again. Cook until the tomatoes are soft.

5. Pour the beaten egg over the veggies in the pan. Do not stir at all. Let it simmer for 50 to 60 seconds.

6. Serve with pita bread, cucumbers, and low fat feta cheese.

Calories	Protein	Carbs	Fat	Fiber
108	3.6 g	14.3 g	5.1 g	3 g

◆→ Mediterranean Pistachios and Fruits with Yogurt ←◆

Servings: 6

Preparation Time: 10 minutes

Cooking Time: 45 minutes

Ingredients:

- ¾ cup of pistachios, unsalted
- ¼ cup of chopped dried apricots
- ⅛ tsp of ground or grated nutmeg
- 1 tsp of raw sugar
- 2 tbsp of dried pomegranate seeds or dried cranberries
- ⅛ tsp of ground allspice
- ¼ tsp of cinnamon
- greek yogurt to serve, as required

Directions:

1. Grease a rimmed baking sheet with cooking spray. Place pistachios on it.
2. Bake in a preheated oven at 350° F for about seven minutes or until nuts are toasted lightly. Remove from the oven and let it cool.
3. Transfer the pistachios into a bowl. Add rest of the ingredients except yogurt. Toss well.
4. Sprinkle salt and pepper to taste.
5. Cover and cook until the eggs are cooked. Do not uncover for at least five minutes.
6. Garnish with parsley and serve over ciabatta rolls.

Calories	Protein	Carbs	Fat	Fiber
116	3.5 g	11 g	7.1 g	2.1 g

Mediterranean Eggs

Servings: 3

Preparation Time: 10 minutes

Cooking Time: 25 minutes

Ingredients:

- 1 medium onion, sliced
- ½ tbsp of extra-virgin olive oil
- 3 tbsp of firmly packed, julienne cut, sun-dried tomatoes
- 1.5 oz of crumbled feta cheese
- chopped parsley, to garnish
- ½ tbsp of butter
- 2 small cloves garlic, minced
- 3 large eggs
- kosher salt to taste
- freshly ground pepper to taste
- crusty ciabatta rolls, to serve

Directions:

1. Place a skillet (preferably cast iron) over medium-low heat. Add butter and oil. When the butter melts, stir in the onions and cook until brown. It can take at least 30 minutes. Stir occasionally.
2. Stir in sun-dried tomatoes and garlic and cook until aromatic. Spread it evenly.
3. Crack eggs at different spots on top. Scatter feta cheese.

Calories	Protein	Carbs	Fat	Fiber
183	9 g	11 g	11 g	1 g

Shakshuka

Servings: 6

Preparation Time: 10 minutes

Cooking Time: 15 minutes

Ingredients:

- 2 medium onions, chopped
- 3 cloves garlic, sliced
- 3 red bell peppers, chopped
- ½ tsp of sugar
- 6 eggs
- 3 tbsp of olive oil
- ½ tsp of spicy harissa peppers
- salt to taste
- pepper to taste
- 1 ½ cans (15 oz each) of diced tomatoes

Directions:

1. Place a heavy bottomed skillet over medium heat. Add oil and let it heat.
2. Stir in the onions and cook until onions are tender. Then add the bell peppers and toss for two minutes.
3. Stir in the garlic and cook for a couple of minutes until aromatic.
4. Place a heavy bottomed skillet over medium heat. Add oil and let it heat.
5. Stir in the onions and cook until onions are tender. Then add the bell peppers and toss for two minutes.
6. Stir in the garlic and cook for a couple of minutes until aromatic.
7. Stir in the tomatoes, harissa peppers, salt, pepper, and sugar. Cook for about five to six minutes.

8. Make six holes in the mixture and crack an egg in each.

9. Cover with a lid and cook until the eggs are cooked.

Nutritional Values Per Serving

Calories	Protein	Carbs	Fat	Fiber
179	7 g	12 g	11 g	2 g

Berry Breakfast Smoothie

Servings: 1

Preparation Time: 10 minutes

Cooking Time: 40 minutes

Ingredients:

o   1 ¼ cups of frozen berries of your choice

o   2 tbsp of milk

o   1 tsp of honey

o   4.4 oz of Greek yogurt

o   1.8 oz of oats

Directions:

1. Toss all ingredients into a blender and blend on high for a minute.

2. Pour into a glass and serve with crushed ice if desired.

Nutritional Values Per Serving

Calories	Protein	Carbs	Fat	Fiber
295	18 g	44 g	5 g	7 g

Mediterranean Diet Smoothie

Servings: 1

Preparation Time: 10 minutes

Cooking Time: 45 minutes

Ingredients:

o   1 cups of loosely packed baby spinach

o   ½ banana, sliced, frozen

o   ¼ inch of fresh ginger, peeled, sliced

o   ½ small mango, peeled, pitted, chopped

o   ¼ cup of skim milk or unsweetened almond milk

o   ½ cup of beet juice

o   ice cubes, as required

Directions:

1.   Toss all ingredients into a blender and blend
on high for a minute.

2.   Pour into a glass and serve with crushed ice

Nutritional Values Per Serving

Calories	Protein	Carbs	Fat	Fiber
168	4 g	39 g	1 g	5 g

Servings: 3

Preparation Time: 10 minutes

Cooking Time: 10 minutes

Ingredients:

- ¼ cup of almond flour
- ½ tsp of ground cinnamon
- 3 eggs
- 1 banana, mashed
- 1 tbsp of almond butter
- 1 tsp of vanilla extract
- 1 tsp of olive oil
- sliced banana to serve

Directions:

1. Whisk the eggs in a mixing bowl until they become fluffy.
2. In another bowl, mash the banana using a fork and add to the egg mixture.
3. Add the vanilla, almond butter, cinnamon and almond flour.
4. Mix into a smooth batter.
5. Heat the olive oil in a skillet.
6. Add one spoonful of the batter and fry them on both sides.
7. Keep doing these steps until you are done with all the batter.
8. Heat the olive oil in a skillet.
9. Add one spoonful of the batter and fry them on both sides.
10. Keep doing these steps until you are done with all the batter.
11. Add some sliced banana on top before serving.

Nutritional Values Per Serving

Calories	Protein	Carbs	Fat
306	14.4 g	3.6 g	26 g

Mediterranean Breakfast Pitas

Servings: 4

Preparation Time: 10 minutes

Cooking Time: 30 minutes

Ingredients:

o   4 big eggs, at room temperature

o   salt

o   2 whole wheat pita breads with pockets, cut down the middle

o   ½ cup of Hummus (4 oz)

o   1 medium cucumber, meagerly cut into adjusts

o   2 medium tomatoes, huge shakers

o   handful of new parsley leaves, coarsely hacked

o   freshly ground dark pepper

o   *hot sauce (discretionary)*

Directions:

1. Fill a medium pot with water and heat to the point of boiling.

2. Tenderly place your room-temperature eggs in the water and cook for 7 minutes.

3. Channel the water and run the eggs under chilly water to cool.

4. Strip the eggs and cut into ¼ inch thick cuts. Sprinkle with salt and put in a safe place.

5. Spread within every pita pocket with 2 tablespoons of hummus.

6. Place a couple of cucumber cuts and some diced tomato into every pita.

7. Sprinkle with salt and pepper.

8. Fold 1 cut egg into every pita and sprinkle with parsley and hot sauce (if utilizing).

Calories	Protein	Carbs	Fat	Saturated	Fiber	Sugars	Sodium
206	12 g (24.1%)	22.9 g (7.6 %)	8.3 g (12.8%)	2.1 g (10.6 %)	4.9 g (19.7%)	3.4 g	564.4 mg (23.5%)

✦ Spinach and Artichoke Frittata ✦

Servings: 4 to 6

Preparation Time: 5 minutes

Cooking Time: 22 to 25 minutes

Ingredients:

- 10 big eggs
- ½ cup of full-fat acrid cream
- 1 tbsp of Dijon mustard
- 1 tsp of genuine salt
- ¼ tsp of crisply ground dark pepper
- 1 cup of ground parmesan cheddar (around 3 oz), divided
- 2 tbsp of olive oil
- about 14 oz of marinated artichoke hearts, depleted, tapped dry, and quartered
- 5 oz of Infant spinach (around 5 pressed cups)
- 2 cloves
- garlic, minced

Directions:

1. Arrange a rack in the broiler and heat to 400° F.

2. Place the eggs, harsh cream, mustard, salt, pepper and ½ cup of the parmesan in a huge bowl and race to consolidate; put in a safe place.

3. Heat the oil in a 10 inch cast iron or broiler safe nonstick skillet over medium heat until gleaming.

4. Include the artichokes in a solitary layer and cook, blending occasionally, until delicately caramelized, 6 to 8 minutes.

5. Include the spinach and garlic, and hurl until the spinach is withered and practically all of the fluid is vanished, around 2 minutes.

6. Spread everything into an even layer.

7. Pour the egg blend over the vegetables.

8. Sprinkle with the staying ½ cup parmesan.

9. Tilt the skillet to ensure the eggs settle uniformly over all the vegetables.

Nutritional Values Per Serving

Based on 6 servings (% day by day esteem)

Calories	Protein	Carbs	Fat	Saturated	Fiber	Sugars	Sodium
316	17.9 g (35.7%)	6.4 g (2.1%)	25.9 g (39.9%)	7.8 g (38.9%)	2.3 g (9.3%)	2.1 g	565.2 mg (23.6%)

Quinoa Pizza Muffins

Servings: 4

Preparation Time: 10 minutes

Cooking Time: 30 minutes

Ingredients:

- 1 cup of uncooked quinoa
- 2 large eggs
- ½ medium onion, diced
- 1 cup of diced bell pepper
- 1 cup of shredded mozzarella cheese
- 1 tbsp of dried basil
- 1 tbsp of dried oregano
- 2 tsp of garlic powder
- ⅛ tsp of salt
- 1 tsp of crushed red peppers
- ½ cup of roasted red pepper, chopped
- pizza sauce, about 1-2 cups

Directions:

1. Preheat oven to 350° F.
2. Cook quinoa according to directions.
3. Combine all ingredients (except sauce) into bowl. Mix all ingredients well.
4. Scoop quinoa pizza mixture into muffin tin evenly. Makes 12 muffins.
5. Bake for 30 minutes until muffins turn golden in color and the edges are getting crispy.
6. Top with 1 or 2 tbsp pizza sauce and enjoy!

Nutritional Values Per Serving

Calories	Protein	Carbs	Fat
303	21 g	41.3 g	6.1 g

Servings: 8

Preparation Time: 10 minutes

Cooking Time: 45 minutes

Ingredients:

- ½ cup of chopped walnuts
- 4 tbsp of fresh, chopped rosemary
- 1 ⅓ cups of lukewarm carbonated water
- 1 tbsp of honey
- ½ cup of extra virgin olive oil
- 1 tsp of apple cider vinegar
- 3 eggs
- 5 tsp of instant dry yeast granules
- 1 tsp of salt
- 1 tbsp of xanthan gum
- ¼ cup of buttermilk powder
- 1 cup of white rice flour
- 1 cup of tapioca starch
- 1 cup of arrowroot starch
- 1 ¼ cups of all-purpose Bob's Red Mill gluten-free flour mix

Directions:

1. In a large mixing bowl, whisk well eggs. Add 1 cup warm water, honey olive oil, and vinegar.
2. While beating continuously, add the rest of the ingredients except for rosemary and walnuts.
3. Continue beating. If dough is too stiff, add a bit of warm water. Dough should be shaggy and thick.
4. Then add rosemary and walnuts continue kneading until evenly distributed.
5. Cover bowl of dough with a clean towel, place in a warm spot, and let it rise for 30 minutes.
6. Fifteen minutes into rising time, preheat oven to 400° F.
7. Generously grease with olive oil a 2 quart Dutch oven and preheat inside oven without the lid.

8. Once dough is done rising, remove pot from oven, and place dough inside. With a wet spatula, spread top of dough evenly in pot.

9. Brush tops of bread with 2 tbsp of olive oil, cover Dutch oven and bake for 35 to 45 minutes.

10. Once bread is done, remove from oven. And gently remove bread from pot.

11. Allow bread to cool at least ten minutes before slicing.

Nutritional Values Per Serving

Calories	Protein	Carbs	Fat
424	7 g	56.8 g	19 g

◆ Banana Coconut Breakfast ◆

Servings: 4

Preparation Time: 10 minutes

Cooking Time: 3 minutes

Ingredients:

○ 1 ripe banana

○ 1 cup of desiccated coconut

○ 1 cup of coconut milk

○ 3 tbsp of raisins, chopped

○ 2 tbsp of ground flax seed

○ 1 tsp of vanilla

○ a dash of cinnamon

○ a dash of nutmeg

○ salt to taste

Directions:

1. Place all ingredients in a deep pan.

2. Allow to simmer for 3 minutes on low heat.

3. Place in individual containers.

4. Put a label and store in the fridge.

5. Allow to thaw at room temperature before heating in the microwave oven.

Nutritional Values Per Serving

Calories	Protein	Carbs	Fat	Fiber
279	6.4 g	25.46 g	8.8 g	5.9 g

CHAPTER 6: VEGETABLES

Basil and Tomato Soup

Servings: 2

Preparation Time: 10 minutes

Cooking Time: 25 minutes

Ingredients:

- salt and pepper to taste
- 2 bay leaves
- 1 ½ cups of almond milk, unsweetened
- ½ tsp of raw apple cider vinegar
- ⅓ cup of basil leaves
- ¼ cup of tomato paste
- 3 cups of tomatoes, chopped
- 1 medium celery stalk, chopped
- 1 medium carrot, chopped
- 1 medium garlic clove, minced
- ½ cup of white onion
- 2 tbsp of vegetable broth

Directions:

1. Heat the vegetable broth in a large saucepan over medium heat.
2. Add the onions and cook for 3 minutes. Add the garlic and cook for another minute.
3. Add the celery and carrots and cook for 1 minute.
4. Mix in the tomatoes and bring to a boil. Simmer for 15 minutes.
5. Add the almond milk, basil and bay leaves. Season with salt and pepper to taste.

Nutritional Values Per Serving

Calories	Protein	Carbs	Fat
213	6.9 g	42 g	3.9 g

Butternut Squash Hummus

Servings: 8

Preparation Time: 10 minutes

Cooking Time: 15 minutes

Ingredients:

- 2 pounds of butternut squash, seeded and peeled
- 1 tbsp of olive oil
- ¼ cup of tahini
- 2 tbsp of lemon juice
- 2 cloves of garlic, minced
- salt and pepper to taste

Directions:

1. Heat the oven to 300° F.
2. Coat the butternut squash with olive oil.
3. Place in a baking dish and bake for 15 minutes in the oven.
4. Once the squash is cooked, place in a food processor together with the rest of the ingredients.
5. Pulse until smooth.
6. Place in individual containers.
7. Put a label and store in the fridge.
8. Allow to warm at room temperature before heating in the microwave oven.
9. Serve with carrots or celery sticks.

Nutritional Values Per Serving

Calories	Protein	Carbs	Fat	Fiber
279	6.4 g	25.46 g	8.8 g	5.9 g

Cajun Jambalaya Soup

Ingredients:

- ¼ cup of Frank's red hot sauce
- 3 tbsp of Cajun seasoning
- 2 cups of okra
- ½ head of cauliflower
- 1 pkg spicy Andouille sausages
- 4 oz of chicken, diced
- 1 lb of large shrimps, raw and deveined
- 2 bay leaves
- 2 cloves of garlic, diced
- 1 large can of organic diced tomatoes
- 1 large onion, chopped
- 4 pepper
- 5 cups of chicken stock

Directions:

1. In slow cooker, place the bay leaves, red hot sauce, Cajun seasoning, chicken, garlic, onions, and peppers.
2. Set slow cooker on low and cook for 5 ½ hours.
3. Then add sausages cook for 10 minutes.
4. Meanwhile, pulse cauliflower in food processor to make cauliflower rice.
5. Add cauliflower rice into slow cooker. Cook for 20 minutes.

Nutritional Values Per Serving

Calories	Protein	Carbs	Fat
155	17.4 g	13.9 g	3.8 g

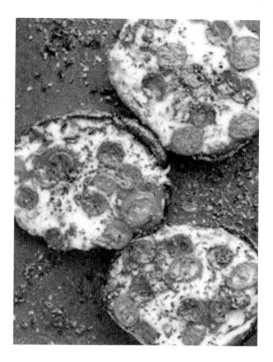

Servings: 4

Preparation Time: 10 minutes

Cooking Time: 12 minutes

Ingredients:

- ½ tsp of red pepper flakes
- a handful of fresh basil, chopped
- 1 can of black olives, chopped
- 1 medium onion, chopped
- 1 green pepper, chopped
- ¼ cup of chopped roasted yellow peppers
- ½ cup of prepared nut cheese, shredded
- 2 cups of prepared gluten-free pizza sauce
- 8 Portobello mushrooms, cleaned and stems removed

Directions:

1. Preheat the oven toaster.
2. Take a baking sheet and grease it. Set aside.
3. Place the Portobello mushroom cap-side down and spoon 2 tablespoon of packaged pizza sauce on the underside of each cap. Add nut cheese and top with the remaining ingredients.
4. Broil for 12 minutes or until the toppings are wilted.

Nutritional Values Per Serving

Calories	Protein	Carbs	Fat
578	24.4 g	73 g	22.4 g

Servings: 6

Preparation Time: 10 minutes

Cooking Time: 1 hour and 30 minutes

Ingredients:

o 2 tbsp of olive oil

o 1 head of garlic, cloves separated and peeled

o 1 large turnip, peeled and cut into ½ inch pieces

o 1 medium sized red onion, cut into ½ inch pieces

o 1 ½ lbs of beets, trimmed but not peeled, scrubbed and cut into ½ inch pieces

o 1 ½ lbs of Yukon gold potatoes, unpeeled, cut into ½ inch pieces

o 2 ½ lbs of butternut squash, peeled, seeded, cut into ½ inch pieces

Directions:

1. Grease 2 rimmed and large baking sheets. Preheat oven to 425° F.

2. In a large bowl, mix all ingredients thoroughly.

3. Into the two baking sheets, evenly divide the root vegetables, spread in one layer.

4. Season generously with pepper and salt.

5. Pop into the oven and roast for 1 hour and 15 minute or until golden brown and tender.

6. Remove from oven and let it cool for at least 15 minutes before serving.

Nutritional Values Per Serving

Calories	Protein	Carbs	Fat
298	7.4 g	61.1 g	5 g

Servings: 4

Preparation Time: 10 minutes

Cooking Time: 15 minutes

Ingredients:

- ¼ cup of chopped fresh mint
- ¼ cup of lemon juice
- ¼ tsp of salt
- ½ cup of bulgur
- ½ tsp of minced garlic
- 1 cup of water
- 1 small cucumber, peeled, seeded and diced
- 2 cups of finely chopped flat-leaf parsley
- 2 tbsp of extra virgin olive oil
- 2 tomatoes, diced
- 4 scallions, thinly sliced
- pepper to taste

Directions:

1. Cook bulgur according to package instructions. Drain and set aside to cool for at least 15 minutes.
2. In a small bowl, mix pepper, salt, garlic, oil, and lemon juice.
3. Transfer bulgur into a large salad bowl and mix in scallions, cucumber, tomatoes, mint, and parsley.
4. Pour in dressing and toss well to coat.
5. Place bowl in ref until chilled before serving.

Nutritional Values Per Serving

Calories	Protein	Carbs	Fat
134.8	7.2 g	13 g	6 g

Ingredients:

- ½ cup of grated Parmigiano Reggiano cheese
- no boil lasagna noodles
- cooking spray
- ¼ cup of all-purpose flour
- 3 cups of reduced fat milk, divided
- 2 tbsp of chopped fresh chives, divided
- ⅓ cup of less fat cream cheese
- ½ cup of white wine
- 6 garlic cloves, minced and divided
- 1 ½ tbsp of chopped fresh thyme
- ½ tsp of freshly ground black pepper, divided
- 1 tsp of salt, divided
- 1 package of 4 oz pre-sliced exotic mushroom blend
- 1 package of 8 oz pre-sliced cremini mushrooms
- 1 ¼ cups of chopped shallots
- 2 tbsp of olive oil, divided
- 1 tbsp of butter
- 1 oz of dried porcini mushrooms
- 1 cup of boiling water

Directions:

1. For 30 minutes, submerge porcini in 1 cup boiling hot water. With a sieve, strain mushroom and reserve liquid.
2. Over medium high fire, melt butter on a fry pan. Mix in 2 tbsp oil and for three minutes fry shallots.
3. Add ¼ tsp pepper, ½ tsp salt, exotic mushrooms and cremini, cook for six minutes.
4. Stir in 3 garlic cloves and thyme, cook for a minute.
5. Bring to a boil as you pour wine by increasing fire to high and cook until liquid evaporates around a minute.
6. Turn off fire and stir in porcini mushrooms, 1 tbsp chives and cream cheese. Mix well.

7. On medium high fire, place a separate medium sized pan with 1 tbsp oil. Sauté for half a minute 3 garlic cloves.

8. Then bring to a boil as you pour 2 ¾ cups milk and reserved porcini liquid. Season with remaining pepper and salt. In a separate bowl, whisk together flour and ¼ cup milk and pour into pan. Stir constantly and cook until mixture thickens.

9. In a greased rectangular glass dish, pour and spread ½ cup of sauce, top with lasagna, top with half of mushroom mixture and another layer of lasagna. Repeat the layering process and instead of lasagna layer, end with the mushroom mixture and cover with cheese.

10. For 45 minutes, bake the lasagna in a preheated 350° F oven. Garnish with chives before serving.

Nutritional Values Per Serving

Calories	Protein	Carbs	Fat
268	10.2 g	29.6 g	12.6 g

Artichokes, Olives & Tuna Pasta

Servings: 4

Preparation Time: 10 minutes

Cooking Time: 15 minutes

Ingredients:

- ¼ cup of chopped fresh basil
- ¼ cup of chopped green olives
- ¼ tsp of freshly ground pepper
- ½ cup of white wine
- ½ tsp of salt, divided
- 1 10 oz package of frozen artichoke hearts, thawed and squeezed dry
- 2 cups of grape tomatoes, halved
- 2 tbsp of lemon juice
- 2 tsp of chopped fresh rosemary
- 2 tsp of freshly grated lemon zest
- 3 cloves of garlic, minced
- 4 tbsp of extra virgin olive oil, divided
- 6 oz of whole wheat penne pasta
- 8 oz of tuna steak, cut into 3 pieces

Directions:

1. Cook penne pasta according to package instructions. Drain and set aside.
2. Preheat grill to medium high.
3. In bowl, toss and mix ¼ tsp pepper, ¼ tsp salt, 1 tsp rosemary, lemon zest, 1 tbsp oil and tuna pieces.
4. Grill tuna for 3 minutes per side. Allow to cool and flake into bite sized pieces.
5. On medium fire, place a large nonstick saucepan and heat 3 tbsp oil.
6. Sauté remaining rosemary, garlic olives, and artichoke hearts for 4 minutes Add wine and tomatoes, bring to a boil and cook for 3 minutes while stirring once in a while.
7. Add remaining salt, lemon juice, tuna pieces and pasta. Cook until heated through.
8. To serve, garnish with basil and enjoy.

Nutritional Values Per Serving

Calories	Protein	Carbs	Fat
127	7.2 g	13 g	5.2 g

CHAPTER 7: POULTRY AND MEAT

Lemon Garlic Chicken

Servings: 6

Preparation Time: 10 minutes

Cooking Time: 1 hour and 20 minutes

Ingredients:

- 6 chicken breast fillets
- 3 tbsp of olive oil
- 1 tbsp of lemon juice
- 3 cloves of garlic, crushed and minced
- 2 tsp of dried parsley

Directions:

1. Marinate the chicken breast fillets in a mixture of olive oil, lemon juice, garlic, parsley, and a pinch of salt and pepper.
2. Let sit for 1 hour covered in the refrigerator.
3. Press the sauté setting in the Instant Pot.
4. Pour in the vegetable oil.
5. Cook the chicken for 5 minutes per side or until fully cooked.

Serving Suggestion: Serve with rice or salad.

Tip: You can also slice the chicken before cooking.

Nutritional Values Per Serving

Calories	Protein	Cholesterol	Total Fat	Saturated Fat
341	42.4 g	130 mg	17.9 g	4 g

Total Carbohydrate	Dietary Fiber	Total Sugars	Potassium	Sodium
0.7 g	0.1 g	0.1 g	368 g	127 mg

Chicken & Rice

Servings: 8

Preparation Time: 10 minutes

Cooking Time: 50 minutes

Ingredients:

- 1 whole chicken, sliced into smaller pieces
- 2 tbsp of dry Greek seasoning
- 1 ½ cups of long grain white rice
- 1 cup of chopped parsley

Directions:

1. Coat the chicken with the seasoning mix.
2. Add 2 cups of water to the Instant Pot and add the chicken inside.
3. Seal the pot and choose manual mode.
4. Cook at high pressure for 30 minutes. Release the pressure naturally.
5. Lift the chicken and place on a baking sheet.
6. Bake in the oven for 5 minutes or until skin is crispy.
7. While waiting, strain the broth from the Instant Pot to remove the chicken residue.
8. Add the rice and seal the pot.
9. Set it to rice function, fluff the rice and serve with the chicken.

Calories	Protein	Cholesterol	Total Fat	Saturated Fat
412	45.1 g	130 mg	11.2 g	3.1 g

Total Carbohydrate	Dietary Fiber	Total Sugars	Potassium	Sodium
29.3 g	0.7 g	0.1 g	450 g	249 mg

◆ Chicken Shawarma ◆

Servings: 8

Preparation Time: 10 minutes

Cooking Time: 30 minutes

Ingredients:

- o 2 lb of chicken breast, sliced into strips
- o 1 tsp of paprika
- o 1 tsp of ground cumin
- o ¼ tsp of granulated garlic
- o ½ tsp of turmeric
- o ¼ tsp of ground allspice

Directions:

1. Season the chicken with the spices, and a little salt and pepper.
2. Pour 1 cup chicken broth to the pot and seal it.
3. Choose poultry setting and cook for 15 minutes.
4. Release the pressure naturally.

Serving Suggestion: Serve with roasted sweet potatoes.

Calories	Protein	Cholesterol	Total Fat	Saturated Fat
132	24.2 g	73 mg	3 g	0 g

Total Carbohydrate	Dietary Fiber	Total Sugars	Potassium	Sodium
0.5 g	0.2 g	0.1 g	435 g	58 mg

◆———→ Mediterranean Chicken ←———◆

Servings: 6

Preparation Time: 10 minutes

Cooking Time: 10 minutes

Ingredients:

- 2 lb of chicken breast fillet, sliced into strips
- wine mixture (¼ cup of white wine mixed with 3 tbsp of red wine)
- 2 tbsp of light brown sugar
- 1 ½ tsp of dried oregano
- 6 garlic cloves, chopped

Directions:

1. Pour in the wine mixture to the Instant Pot.
2. Stir in the rest of the ingredients.
3. Toss the chicken to coat evenly.
4. Seal the pot and set it to high pressure.
5. Cook for 10 minutes and release the pressure naturally.

Serving Suggestion: Serve with white rice.

Nutritional Values Per Serving

Calories	Protein	Cholesterol	Total Fat	Saturated Fat
304	44 g	73 mg	11.3 g	3.1 g

Total Carbohydrate	Dietary Fiber	Total Sugars	Potassium	Sodium
4.2 g	0.2 g	3 g	390 g	131 mg

Lime Chicken with Black Beans

Servings: 8

Preparation Time: 10 minutes

Cooking Time: 30 minutes

Ingredients:

o 8 chicken thighs (boneless and skinless)

o 3 tbsp of lime juice

o 1 cup of black beans

o 1 cup of canned tomatoes

o 4 tsp of garlic powder

Directions:

1. Marinate the chicken in a mixture of lime juice and garlic powder.

2. Add the chicken to the Instant Pot and pour the tomatoes on top of the chicken.

3. Seal the pot and set it to manual.

4. Cook at high pressure for 10 minutes.

5. Release the pressure naturally and stir in the black beans.

6. Press sauté to simmer until black beans are cooked.

Serving Suggestion: Serve with rice or salad.

Nutritional Values Per Serving

Calories	Protein	Cholesterol	Total Fat	Saturated Fat
370	47.9 g	130 mg	11.2 g	3.1 g

Total Carbohydrate	Dietary Fiber	Total Sugars	Potassium	Sodium
17.5 g	4.1 g	1.5 g	790 g	128 mg

Mediterranean Chicken Wings

Servings: 4

Preparation Time: 10 minutes

Cooking Time: 1 hour and 20 minutes

Ingredients:

o 8 chicken wings

o 1 tbsp of garlic puree

o 2 tbsp of mixed dried herbs (tarragon, oregano and basil)

o 1 tbsp of chicken seasoning

Directions:

1. In a bowl, mix the garlic puree, herbs and seasoning.

2. Marinate the chicken in this mixture for 1 hour.

3. Add 1 tablespoon of coconut oil into the Instant Pot and set it to sauté.

4. Cook the chicken until brown on both sides; remove and set aside.

5. Add 1 cup of water to the pot and place steamer basket inside.

6. Put the chicken on top of the basket and seal the pot.

7. Set it to manual and cook at high pressure for 10 minutes.

8. Release the pressure naturally.

Serving Suggestion: Serve with fresh green salad.

Tip: You can also use minced garlic in place of garlic puree.

Nutritional Values Per Serving

Calories	Protein	Cholesterol	Total Fat	Saturated Fat
280	42.2 g	130 mg	11.2 g	3 g

Total Carbohydrate	Dietary Fiber	Total Sugars	Potassium	Sodium
0 g	0	0 g	355 g	135 mg

◆— Honey Balsamic Chicken ◆

Servings: 10

Preparation Time: 10 minutes

Cooking Time: 1 hour

Ingredients:

o ¼ cup of honey

o ½ cup of balsamic vinegar

o ¼ cup of soy sauce

o 2 cloves of garlic minced

o 10 chicken drumsticks

Directions:

1. Mix the honey, vinegar, soy sauce and garlic in a bowl.

2. Marinate the chicken in the sauce for 30 minutes and cover the pot, setting it to manual.

3. Cook at high pressure for 10 minutes.

3. Cook at high pressure for 10 minutes.

4. Release the pressure quickly.

5. Choose the sauté button to thicken the sauce.

Serving Suggestion: Garnish with lemon wedges.

Tip: You can also use chicken wings or other chicken parts for this recipe.

Nutritional Values Per Serving

Calories	Protein	Cholesterol	Total Fat	Saturated Fat
184	21.9 g	67 mg	4.4 g	1.2 g

Total Carbohydrate	Dietary Fiber	Total Sugars	Potassium	Sodium
13 g	0.1 g	11.9 g	202 g	662 mg

◆ Beef Corn Chili ◆

Servings: 8

Preparation Time: 8-10 minutes

Cooking Time: 30 minutes

Ingredients:

o   2 small onions, chopped (finely)

o   ¼ cup of canned corn

o   1 tbsp of oil

o   10 oz of lean ground beef

o   2 small chili peppers, diced

Directions:

1. Take your instant pot and place over dry kitchen surface; open its top lid and switch it on. Press "SAUTE". In its Cooking pot, add and heat the oil. Add the onions, chili pepper, and beef; cook for 2-3 minutes until turn translucent and softened.

2. Add the 3 cups water in the Cooking pot; combine to mix well.

3. Close its top lid and make sure that its valve it closed to avoid spilling.

4. Press "MEAT/STEW". Adjust the timer to 20 minutes.

5. Press will slowly build up; let the added ingredients to cook until the timer indicates zero.

6. Press "CANCEL". Now press "NPR" for natural release pressure. Instant pot will gradually release pressure for about 8-10 minutes. Open the top lid; transfer the cooked recipe in serving plates.

7. Serve the recipe warm.

Nutritional Values Per Serving

Calories	Protein	Fat	Carbs
94	7 g	5 g	2 g

◆ Balsamic Beef Dish ◆

Servings: 8

Preparation Time: 5 minutes

Cooking Time: 55 minutes

Ingredients:

- 3 pounds of chuck roast
- 3 cloves of garlic, thinly sliced
- 1 tbsp of oil
- 1 tsp of flavored vinegar
- ½ tsp of pepper
- ½ tsp of rosemary
- 1 tbsp of butter
- ½ tsp of thyme
- ¼ cup of balsamic vinegar
- 1 cup of beef broth

Directions:

1. Cut slits in the roast and stuff garlic slices all over.
2. Take a bowl and add flavored vinegar, rosemary, pepper, thyme and rub the mixture over the roast.
3. Set your pot to sauté mode and add oil, allow the oil to heat up.
4. Add roast and brown both sides (5 minutes each side).
5. Take the roast out and keep it on the side.
6. Add butter, broth, balsamic vinegar and deglaze the pot.
7. Transfer the roast back and lock up the lid, cook on HIGH pressure for 40 minutes.
8. Perform a quick release, remove the lid and serve!

Nutritional Values Per Serving

Calories	Protein	Fat	Carbs
393	37 g	15 g	25 g

Soy Sauce Beef Roast

Servings: 2-3

Preparation Time: 5-8 minutes

Cooking Time: 35 minutes

Ingredients:

o ½ tsp of beef bouillon

o 1 ½ tsp of rosemary

o ½ tsp of minced garlic

o 2 pounds of roast beef

o ⅓ cup of soy sauce

Directions:

1. Mix the soy sauce, bouillon, rosemary, and garlic together in a mixing bowl.

2. Place your instant pot over as dry kitchen platform. Open the top lid and plug it on.

3. Add the roast, bowl mix and enough water to cover the roast; gently stir to mix well.

4. Properly close the top lid; make sure that the safety valve is properly locked.

5. Press "MEAT/STEW" Cooking function; set pressure level to "HIGH" and set the Cooking time to 35 minutes.

6. Allow the pressure to build to cook the ingredients.

7. After Cooking time is over press "CANCEL" setting. Find and press "NPR" Cooking function. This setting is for the natural release of inside pressure, and it takes around 10 minutes to slowly release pressure.

8. Slowly open the lid, take out the cooked meat and shred it.

9. Add the shredded meat back in the potting mix and stir to mix well.

10. Take out the cooked recipe in serving containers. Serve warm.

Nutritional Values Per Serving

Calories	Protein	Fat	Carbs
423	21 g	14 g	12 g

Rosemary Beef Chuck Roast

Servings: 5-6

Preparation Time: 5 minutes

Cooking Time: 45 minutes

Ingredients:

- 3 pounds of chuck beef roast
- 3 garlic cloves
- ¼ cup of balsamic vinegar
- 1 sprig of fresh rosemary
- 1 sprig of fresh thyme
- 1 cup of water
- 1 tbsp of vegetable oil
- salt and pepper to taste

Directions:

1. Cut slices in the beef roast and place the garlic cloves in them.
2. Coat the roast with the herbs, black pepper, and salt.
3. Preheat your instant pot using the sauté setting and add the oil.
4. When warmed, add the beef roast and stir-cook until browned on all sides.
5. Add the remaining ingredients; stir gently. Seal the lid and cook on high pressure for 40 minutes using the manual setting. Let the pressure release naturally, about 10 minutes.
6. Uncover the instant pot; transfer the beef roast the serving plates, slice and serve.

Calories	Protein	Fat	Carbs
542	55.2 g	11.2 g	8.7 g

Pork Chops and Tomato Sauce

Servings: 4

Preparation Time: 10 minutes

Cooking Time: 20 minutes

Ingredients:

- 4 pork chops, boneless
- 1 tbsp of soy sauce
- ¼ tsp of sesame oil
- 1 and ½ cups of tomato paste
- 1 yellow onion
- 8 mushrooms, sliced

Directions:

1. In a bowl, mix pork chops with soy sauce and sesame oil, toss and leave aside for 10 minutes.
2. Set your instant pot on sauté mode, add pork chops and brown them for 5 minutes on each side.
3. Add onion, stir and cook for 1-2 minutes more.
4. Add tomato paste and mushrooms, toss, cover and cook on high for 8-9 minutes.
5. Divide everything between plates and serve.

Nutritional Values Per Serving

Calories	Protein	Fat	Carbs
300	4 g	7 g	18 g

◆ Pork Potato ◆

Servings: 4

Preparation Time: 8-10 minutes

Cooking Time: 25 minutes

Ingredients:

o   10 oz of pork neck, remove fat and make small pieces

o   1 medium sweet potato, chopped

o   1 tbsp of oil

o   3 cups of beef stock

o   1 onion, chopped (finely)

Directions:

1. Take your pot and place over dry kitchen surface; open its top lid and switch it on.
2. Press "SAUTÉ". Grease the pot with some cooking oil.
3. Add the onions; cook for 2 minutes until turn translucent and softened.
4. Add the meat; stir-cook for 4-5 minutes to evenly brown.
5. Mix in the stock and potatoes.
6. Close its top lid and make sure that its valve it closed to avoid spillage.
7. Press "MANUAL". Adjust the timer to 20 minutes.
8. Pressure will slowly build up; let the added ingredients to cook until the timer indicates zero.
9. Press "CANCEL". Now press "NPR" for natural release pressure. Instant pot will gradually release pressure for about 8-10 minutes.
10. Open the top lid and transfer the cooked recipe in serving plates.
11. Serve the recipe warm.

Nutritional Values Per Serving

Calories	Protein	Fat	Carbs
278	18 g	18 g	12 g

❖ Coffee Flavored Pork Ribs ❖

Servings: 4

Preparation Time: 3 minutes

Cooking Time: 40 minutes

Ingredients:

- o 1 rack of baby back ribs
- o 2 tsp of sesame oil
- o 3 tbsp of oyster sauce
- o 1 tsp of salt
- o 1 tsp of sugar
- o 1 cup of water
- o ½ cup of liquid smoke
- o 2 tbsp of instant coffee powder

Directions:

1. Add the listed ingredients to the pot.
2. Lock the lid and cook on "MEAT/STEW" mode for 40 minutes.
3. Release the pressure naturally over 10 minutes.
4. Serve and enjoy!

Nutritional Values Per Serving

Calories	Protein	Fat	Carbs
898	77 g	63 g	4 g

Tomato Pork Paste

Servings: 4

Preparation Time: 5-8 minutes

Cooking Time: 15 minutes

Ingredients:

- 2 cups of tomato puree
- 1 tbsp of red wine
- 1 pound of lean ground pork
- 8-10 oz of pack paste of your choice, uncooked
- salt and black pepper to taste
- 1 tbsp of vegetable oil

Directions:

1. Season the pork with black pepper and salt.
2. Place your instant pot over a dry kitchen platform. Open the top lid and plug it on.
3. Press "SAUTE" Cooking function; add the oil and heat it.
4. In the pot, add the ground meat; stir-cook using wooden spatula until turns evenly brown for 8-10 minutes.
5. Add the wine. Cook for 1-2 minutes.
6. Add the ingredients; gently stir to mix well.
7. Properly close the top lid; make sure that the safety valve is properly locked.
8. Press "MEAT/STEW" Cooking function; set pressure level to "HIGH" and set the Cooking time to 6 minutes.
9. Allow the pressure to build to cook the ingredients.
10. After Cooking time is over press "CANCEL" setting. Find and press "NPR" Cooking function. This setting is for the natural release of inside pressure, and it takes around 10 minutes to slowly release pressure.
11. Slowly open the lid, take out the cooked recipe in serving containers. Serve warm.

Nutritional Values Per Serving

Calories	Protein	Fat	Carbs
423	36 g	34 g	14 g

◆ Garlic Pulled Pork ◆

Servings: 12

Preparation Time: 5 minutes

Cooking Time: 1 hour and 35/40 minutes

Ingredients:

- 4 pounds of pork shoulder, boneless and cut into 3 pieces
- 2 tbsp of soy sauce
- 2 tbsp of brown sugar
- 1 cup of chicken broth
- 10 cloves of garlic, finely chopped
- 2 tbsp of butter, melted at room temperature

Directions:

1. In a mixing bowl, combine the broth, soy sauce and brown sugar. Add the garlic and stir to combine. Preheat your instant pot using the sauté setting and add the butter.
2. When warmed, add the pork pieces and stir-cook until browned on all sides.
3. Add the soy mix; stir gently.
4. Seal the lid and cook on high pressure for 90 minutes using the manual setting.
5. Let the pressure release naturally, about 10 minutes.
6. Uncover the instant pot; take out the meat and shred it using a fork.
7. Return the shredded meat to the instant pot and stir the mixture well.
8. Transfer to serving plates and serve.

Nutritional Values Per Serving

Calories	Protein	Fat	Carbs
142	11.2 g	8.2 g	3.5 g

⟵ Simple Lamb Ribs and Sauce ⟶

Servings: 2

Preparation Time: 10 minutes

Cooking Time: 30 minutes

Ingredients:

- 4 lamb ribs
- 1 carrot, chopped
- 6 oz of veggie stock
- 1 tbsp of olive oil
- 1 tbsp of white flour

Directions:

1. Set your instant pot on sauté mode, add the oil, heat it up, add lamb and brown it for a few minutes on all sides.
2. Add flour, carrot and stock stir, cover the pot, and cook on high for 20 minutes.
3. Serve lamb with carrots on the side and Cooking juice drizzled all over.

Nutritional Values Per Serving

Calories	Protein	Fat	Carbs
200	25 g	4 g	14 g

Rosemary Lamb

Servings: 7-8

Preparation Time: 8-10 minutes

Cooking Time: 50 minutes

Ingredients:

- o 2 onions, chopped
- o 2 rosemary sprigs
- o 3 cups of beef broth, low-sodium
- o 2 lamb shanks, about 1 pound each
- o 2 bay leaves

Directions:

1. Take your instant pot and place over dry kitchen surface; open its top lid and switch it on.

2. Press "SAUTE". Grease the pot with some Cooking oil.

3. Add the meat; stir-cook for 4-5 minutes to evenly brown. Set aside.

4. Add the onions; cook for 3-4 minutes until turn translucent and softened.

5. Add the meat and pour in the broth.

6. Add the remaining ingredients and stir well.

7. Close its top and make sure that its valve it closed to avoid spillage.

8. Press "MANUAL". Adjust the timer to 40 minutes.

9. Pressure will slowly build up; let the added ingredients to cook until the timer indicates zero.

10. Press "CANCEL". Now press "QPR" to quickly release pressure.

11. Open the top lid; transfer the cooked recipe in serving plates.

12. Remove the rosemary spring and bay leaves. Serve the recipe warm.

Calories	*Protein*	*Fat*	*Carbs*
318	37 g	17 g	3 g

Lamb Shanks Curry

Servings: 5

Preparation Time: 10 minutes

Cooking Time: 45 minutes

Ingredients:

- 3 pounds of lamb shanks
- Kosher flavored vinegar
- fresh ground black pepper
- 2 tbsp of ghee
- 2 medium carrots, roughly chopped
- 2 celery, chopped
- 1 large onion, chopped
- 1 tbsp of tomato paste
- 3 cloves, peeled and smashed
- 1 cup of bone broth
- 1 tsp of red boat fish sauce
- 1 tbsp of vinegar

Directions:

1. Season the shanks with pepper and flavored vinegar. Set your pot to sauté mode and add ghee, allow the ghee to melt and heat up.
2. Add shanks and cook for 8-10 minutes until a nice brown texture appears.
3. In the meantime, chop the vegetables.
4. Once you have a nice brown texture on your lamb, remove it from the instant pot and keep it on the side. Add vegetable and season with flavored vinegar and pepper.
5. Add a tablespoon of ghee and mix.
6. Add vegetables, garlic clove, and tomato paste and give it a nice stir.
7. Add shanks and pour broth, vinegar, fish sauce. Sprinkle a bit of pepper and lock up the lid.

8. Cook on HIGH pressure naturally over 45 minutes. Release the pressure naturally over 10 minutes.

9. Serve the shanks and enjoy!

Nutritional Values Per Serving

Calories	Protein	Fat	Carbs
377	13 g	16 g	10 g

Lamb Coconut Curry

Servings: 4-5

Preparation Time: 5-8 minutes

Cooking Time: 15 minutes

Ingredients:

o 2 pounds of lamb, diced

o a small bunch of lemongrass stalks, trimmed and diced

o 4 tbsp of minced chili

o 1 inch of pieces ginger root, chopped

o 1 cup of coconut milk

Directions:

1. Blend the lemongrass, ginger, and chili in a blender to make a paste.

2. Place your instant pot over a dry kitchen platform. Open the top lid and plug it on.

3. Add the paste, lamb, and coconut milk; gently stir to mix well.

4. Properly close the top lid; make sure that the safety valve is properly locked.

5. Press "MEAT/STEW" Cooking function; set pressure level to "HIGH" and set the Cooking time to 15 minutes.

6. Allow the pressure to build to cook the ingredients.

7. After Cooking time is over press "CANCEL" setting. Find and press "QPR" Cooking function. This setting is for quick release of inside pressure.

8. Slowly open the lid, take out the cooked recipe in serving containers. Serve warm.

Nutritional Values Per Serving

Calories	Protein	Fat	Carbs
524	31 g	19 g	28 g

CHAPTER 8: LUNCH

Crispy Black-Eyed Peas

Servings: 6

Preparation Time: 10 minutes

Cooking Time: 15 minutes

Ingredients:

- 15 oz of black-eyed peas
- ⅛ tsp of chipotle chili powder
- ¼ tsp of salt
- ½ tsp of chili powder
- ⅛ tsp of black pepper

Directions:

1. Rinse the beans well with running water then set aside. In a large bowl, mix the spices until well combined.
2. Add the peas to spices and mix.
3. Place the peas in the wire basket and cook for 10 minutes at 360° F.

Nutritional Values Per Serving

Calories	Protein	Fat	Carbs
262	9.2 g	9.4 g	8.6 g

Lemony Green Beans

Servings: 4

Preparation Time: 12 minutes

Cooking Time: 15 minutes

Ingredients:

o   1 lb of green beans washed and destemmed

o   sea salt and black pepper to taste

o   1 lemon

o   ¼ tsp of extra virgin olive oil

Directions:

1. Preheat your air fryer to 400° F and place the green beans in the air fryer basket.

2. Squeeze lemon over beans and season with salt and pepper.

3. Cover ingredients with oil and toss well.

4. Cook green beans for 12 minutes and serve!

Nutritional Values Per Serving

Calories	Protein	Fat	Carbs
263	8.7 g	9.2 g	8.6 g

Roasted Orange Cauliflower

Servings: 2

Preparation Time: 20 minutes

Cooking Time: 15 minutes

Ingredients:

o   1 head of cauliflower

o   ½ lemon, juiced

o   ½ tbsp of olive oil

o   1 tsp of curry powder

o   sea salt and black pepper to taste

Directions:

1. Prepare your cauliflower by washing and removing the leaves and core. Slice it into florets of comparable size.

2. Grease your air fryer with oil and preheat it for 2 minutes at 390° F.

3. Combine fresh lemon juice and curry powder, add the cauliflower florets and stir. Use salt and pepper as seasoning and stir again.

4. Cook for 20 minutes and serve warm.

Nutritional Values Per Serving

Calories	Protein	Cholesterol	Total Fat	Saturated Fat
117	3 g	0 mg	7 g	1 g

Total Carbohydrate	Dietary Fiber	Total Sugars	Sodium
12 g	4 g	7 g	101 mg

Eggplant Parmesan Panini

Servings: 2

Preparation Time: 25 minutes

Cooking Time: 15 minutes

Ingredients:

- 1 medium eggplant, cut into ½ inch slices
- ½ cup of mayonnaise
- 2 tbsp of milk
- black pepper to taste
- ½ tsp of garlic powder
- ½ tsp of onion powder
- 1 tbsp of dried parsley
- ½ cup of breadcrumbs
- ½ tsp of Italian seasoning
- sea salt to taste
- fresh basil, chopped for garnishing
- ¾ cup of tomato sauce
- 2 tbsp of parmesan, grated cheese
- 2 cups of grated mozzarella cheese
- 2 tbsp of olive oil
- 4 slices of artisan Italian bread
- cooking spray

Directions:

1. Cover both sides of eggplant with salt. Place them between sheets of paper towels.
2. Set aside for 30 minutes to get rid of excess moisture.
3. In a mixing bowl, combine Italian seasoning, breadcrumbs, parsley, onion powder, garlic powder and season with salt and pepper. In another small bowl, whisk mayonnaise and milk until smooth.
4. Preheat your air fryer to 400° F. Remove the excess salt from eggplant slices.
5. Cover both sides of eggplant with mayonnaise mixture.
6. Press the eggplant slices into the breadcrumb mixture and use cooking spray on both sides them.
7. Air fry slices in batches for 15 minutes, turning over when halfway done. Each bread slice must be greased with olive oil.
8. On a cutting board, place two slices of bread with oiled sides down. Layer mozzarella cheese and grated parmesan cheese. Place eggplant on cheese.

9. Cover with tomato sauce and add remaining mozzarella and parmesan cheeses. Garnish with chopped fresh basil.

10. Put the second slice of bread oiled side up on top.

11. Take preheated Panini press and place sandwiches on it. Close the lid and cook for 10 minutes.

12. Slice panini into halves and serve.

Nutritional Values Per Serving

Calories	Protein	Fat	Carbs
267	8.5 g	11.3 g	8.7 g

Spinach Samosa

Servings: 2

Preparation Time: 15 minutes

Cooking Time: 15 minutes

Ingredients:

o 1 ½ cups of almond flour

o ½ tsp of baking soda

o 1 tsp of garam masala

o 1 tsp of coriander, chopped

o ¼ cup of green peas

o ½ tsp of sesame seeds

o ¼ cup of potatoes, boiled, small chunks

o 2 tbsp of olive oil

o ¾ cup of boiled and blended spinach puree

o salt and chili powder to taste

Directions:

1. In a bowl, mix baking soda, salt, and flour to make the dough.

2. Add 1 tablespoon of oil and the spinach puree and mix until the dough is smooth.

3. Place in fridge for 20 minutes.

4. In the pan add one tablespoon of oil, then add potatoes, peas and cook for 5 minutes. Add the sesame seeds, garam masala, coriander, and stir.

5. Knead the dough and make the small ball using a rolling pin.

6. Form balls, make into cone shapes, which are then filled with stuffing that is not yet fully cooked.

7. Make sure flour sheets are well sealed.

8. Preheat air fryer to 390° F and place samosas in the air fryer basket and cook for 10 minutes.

Nutritional Values Per Serving

Calories	Protein	Fat	Carbs
254	10.2 g	12.2 g	9.3 g

Avocado Fries

Servings: 4

Preparation Time: 10 minutes

Cooking Time: 15 minutes

Ingredients:

- 1 oz of Aquafina
- 1 avocado, sliced
- ½ tsp of salt
- ½ cup of panko breadcrumbs

Directions:

1. Toss the panko breadcrumbs and salt together in a bowl.
2. Pour Aquafina into another bowl.
3. Dredge the avocado slices in Aquafina and then panko breadcrumbs.
4. Arrange the slices in single layer in air fryer basket and air fry at 390° F for 10 minutes.

Nutritional Values Per Serving

Calories	Protein	Fat	Carbs
263	8.2 g	7.4 g	6.5 g

◆ Honey Roasted Carrots ◆

Servings: 2

Preparation Time: 12 minutes

Cooking Time: 15 minutes

Ingredients:

- 1 tbsp of honey
- salt and pepper to taste
- 3 cups of baby carrots
- 1 tbsp of olive oil

Directions:

1. In a mixing bowl, combine carrots, honey, and olive oil.
2. Season with salt and pepper.
3. Cook in air fryer at 390° F for 12 minutes.

Nutritional Values Per Serving

Calories	Protein	Fat	Carbs
257	7.3 g	11.6 g	8.7 g

◆ Crispy & Crunchy Baby Corn ◆

Servings: 4

Preparation Time: 10 minutes

Cooking Time: 15 minutes

Ingredients:

- 1 cup of almond flour
- 1 tsp of garlic powder
- ¼ tsp of chili powder
- 4 baby corns, boiled
- salt to taste
- ½ tsp of carom seeds
- pinch of baking soda

Directions:

1. In a bowl, add flour, chili powder, garlic powder, baking soda, carom seed, and salt. Mix well.
2. Pour a little water into the batter to make a nice batter.
3. Dip boiled baby corn into the batter to coat.
4. Preheat your air fryer to 350° F.
5. Line the air fryer basket with foil and place the baby corns on foil.
6. Cook baby corns for 10 minutes.

Nutritional Values Per Serving

Calories	Protein	Fat	Carbs
243	10.3 g	9.6 g	8.2 g

❖ Tasty Tofu ❖

Servings: 4

Preparation Time: 12 minutes

Cooking Time: 15 minutes

Ingredients:

o ¼ cup of cornmeal

o 15 oz of extra firm tofu, drained, cubed

o salt and pepper to taste

o 1 tsp of chili flakes

o ¾ cup of cornstarch

Directions:

1. Line the air fryer basket with aluminum foil and brush with oil.

2. Preheat your air fryer to 370° F.

3. Mix all ingredients in a bowl.

4. Place in air fryer and cook for 12 minutes.

Nutritional Values Per Serving

Calories	Protein	Fat	Carbs
246	7.6 g	11.2 g	8.7 g

Crispy Herb Cauliflower Florets

Servings: 2

Preparation Time: 20 minutes

Cooking Time: 15 minutes

Ingredients:

- 1 egg, beaten
- 2 tbsp of parmesan cheese, grated
- 2 cups of cauliflower florets, boiled
- ¼ cup of almond flour
- 1 tbsp olive oil
- salt to taste
- ½ tbsp of mixed herbs
- ½ tsp of chili powder
- ½ tsp of garlic powder
- ½ cup of breadcrumbs

Directions:

1. In a bowl, combine garlic powder, breadcrumbs, chili powder, mixed herbs, salt, and cheese.
2. Add olive oil to the breadcrumb mixture and mix well.
3. Place flour in a bowl and place the egg in another bowl.
4. Dip the cauliflower florets into the beaten egg, then in flour, and coat with breadcrumbs.
5. Preheat your air fryer to 350° F.
6. Place the coated cauliflower florets inside air fryer basket and cook for 20 minutes.

Nutritional Values Per Serving

Calories	Protein	Fat	Carbs
253	8.5 g	11.3 g	9.5 g

Ingredients:

- o   4 ears of corn
- o   salt and pepper to taste
- o   3 tsp of vegetable oil

Directions:

1. Remove the husks from corn, wash and pat them dry.
2. Cut if needed to fit into air fryer basket.
3. Drizzle with vegetable oil and season with salt and pepper.
4. Cook at 400° F for 10 minutes.

Nutritional Values Per Serving

Calories	Protein	Fat	Carbs
256	9.2 g	9.4 g	8.7 g

Spicy Nuts

Ingredients:

- 2 cups of mixed nuts
- 1 tsp of chipotle chili powder
- 1 tsp of salt
- 1 tsp of pepper
- 1 tbsp of butter, melted
- 1 tsp of ground cumin

Directions:

1. In a bowl, add all ingredients and toss to coat.
2. Preheat your air fryer to 350° F for 5 minutes.
3. Add mixed nuts into air fryer basket and roast for 4 minutes.

Nutritional Values Per Serving

Calories	Protein	Fat	Carbs
252	8.4 g	8.6 g	7.2 g

Mediterranean Veggie Mix

Ingredients:

- 1 large zucchini, sliced
- 1 green pepper, sliced
- 1 large parsnip, peeled and cubed
- salt and black pepper to taste
- 2 tbsp of honey
- 2 cloves of garlic, crushed
- 1 tsp of mixed herbs
- 1 tsp of mustard
- 6 tbsp of olive oil, divided
- 4 cherry tomatoes
- 1 medium carrot, peeled and cubed

Directions:

1. Add the zucchini, green pepper, parsnip, cherry tomatoes, carrot to bottom of air fryer.
2. Cover ingredients with 3 tablespoons of oil and adjust the time to 15 minutes. Cook at 360° F.
3. Prepare your marinade by combining remaining ingredients in air fryer safe baking dish.
4. Combine marinade and vegetables in baking dish and stir well. Sprinkle with salt and pepper.
5. Cook it at 390° F for 5 minutes.

Nutritional Values Per Serving

Calories	Protein	Fat	Carbs
262	7.4 g	11.3 g	9.5 g

CHAPTER 9: FISH AND SEAFOOD

Shrimp with Tomatoes & Feta

Servings: 4

Preparation Time: 20 minutes

Cooking Time: 15 minutes

Ingredients:

o   2 tbsp of butter

o   1 tbsp of garlic, minced

o   1 lb of shrimp, peeled and deveined

o   14 oz of canned crushed tomatoes

o   1 cup of feta cheese, crumbled

Directions:

1.   Set the Instant Pot to sauté. Add the butter and wait for it to melt.

2.   Add the garlic and cook until fragrant.

3.   Add the shrimp and tomatoes.

4.   Seal the pot. Set it to manual and cook at low pressure for 1 minute.

5.   Release the pressure quickly. Top with the feta cheese.

Serving Suggestion: Serve with whole wheat toasted bread.

Tip: You can also top with olives.

Nutritional Values Per Serving

Calories	Protein	Cholesterol	Total Fat	Saturated Fat
218	22.5 g	192 mg	10.5 g	6.6 g

Total Carbohydrate	Dietary Fiber	Total Sugars	Potassium	Sodium
7.9 g	2.2 g	4.7 g	150 g	618 mg

Fish Stew with Tomatoes & Olives

Servings: 4

Preparation Time: 15 minutes

Cooking Time: 25 minutes

Ingredients:

- 1 ½ lb of halibut fillet
- 4 cloves of garlic, minced
- 1 cup of cherry tomatoes, sliced in half
- 3 cups of tomato soup
- 1 cup of green olives, pitted and sliced

Directions:

1. Season the fish with salt and pepper.
2. Pour 1 tablespoon olive oil into the Instant Pot. Add the garlic and cook until fragrant.
3. Add the fish and cook for 3 minutes per side.
4. Add the rest of the ingredients.
5. Cover the pot. Select manual function and cook at low pressure for 3 minutes.
6. Release the pressure quickly.

Serving Suggestion: Drizzle with olive oil and sprinkle with chopped fresh cilantro.

Tip: You can also sprinkle herbs on both sides of fish fillet.

Calories	Protein	Cholesterol	Total Fat	Saturated Fat
245	26.3 g	35 mg	3.7 g	0.6 g

Total Carbohydrate	Dietary Fiber	Total Sugars	Potassium	Sodium
28 g	2.9 g	16.5 g	1040 g	1098 mg

◆ Rosemary Salmon ◆

Servings: 3

Preparation Time: 20 minutes

Cooking Time: 25 minutes

Ingredients:

o   1 lb of salmon fillets

o   10 oz of fresh asparagus

o   1 sprig of fresh rosemary

o   ½ cup of cherry tomatoes, sliced in half

Dressing: (mixture of 1 tbsp of olive oil and 1 tbsp lemon juice)

Directions:

1. Add 1 cup of water into the Instant Pot. Place the steamer rack inside.
2. Put the salmon fillets on the rack. Add the rosemary and asparagus on top of the salmon.
3. Cover the pot. Select manual setting and cook at high pressure for 3 minutes.
4. Release the pressure quickly.
5. Transfer to a plate. Place the tomatoes on the side.
6. Drizzle with the dressing.

Serving Suggestion: Garnish with lemon slices.

Nutritional Values Per Serving

Calories	Protein	Cholesterol	Total Fat	Saturated Fat
267	31.7 g	67 mg	14.3 g	2.1 g

Total Carbohydrate	Dietary Fiber	Total Sugars	Potassium	Sodium
5.2 g	2.5 g	2.7 g	853 g	71 mg

Salmon with Tahini Sauce

Servings: 2

Preparation Time: 10 minutes

Cooking Time: 25 minutes

Ingredients:

o   1 lb of salmon fillets

o   3 tbsp of tahini sauce

o   2 lemon slices

o   2 sprigs of fresh rosemary

Directions:

1. Add the water to the Instant Pot.
2. Place a steamer basket inside. Put the salmon on top of the basket.
3. Season with salt and pepper. Place rosemary and lemon slice on top.
4. Cover the pot. Set it to manual and cook at high pressure for 3 minutes.
5. Release the pressure quickly.
6. Drizzle the tahini sauce on top before serving.

Nutritional Values Per Serving

Calories	Protein	Cholesterol	Total Fat	Saturated Fat
306	44.1 g	100 mg	14.2 g	2.1 g

Total Carbohydrate	Dietary Fiber	Total Sugars	Potassium	Sodium
1.4 g	0.7 g	0.2 g	892 g	101 mg

Sautéed Shrimp with Garlic Couscous

Servings: 4

Preparation Time: 10 minutes

Cooking Time: 25 minutes

Ingredients:

o   1 lb of shrimp, peeled and deveined
o   ½ cup of fresh chives, chopped
o   ½ cup of fresh parsley, chopped
o   1 tbsp of scallions, chopped
o   10 oz of garlic flavored couscous

Directions:

1. Choose sauté function in the Instant Pot. Add 2 tablespoons of olive oil.

2. Add the shrimp and herbs, cook for 3 minutes, stirring frequently. Serve with the couscous.

Serving Suggestion: Serve with pasta or rice.

Tip: You can also use plain couscous if you like.

Nutritional Values Per Serving

Calories	Protein	Cholesterol	Total Fat	Saturated Fat
615	43.8 g	239 mg	8.3 g	0.6 g

Total Carbohydrate	Dietary Fiber	Total Sugars	Potassium	Sodium
95 g	8 g	2.7 g	256 g	1556 mg

Salmon with Garlic & Basil Potatoes

Servings: 4

Preparation Time: 10 minutes

Cooking Time: 25 minutes

Ingredients:

- o 1 lb of baby potatoes
- o 4 tbsp of butter, divided
- o 4 salmon fillets
- o 4 cloves of garlic, minced
- o 1 tsp of dried basil

Directions:

1. Put the potatoes in the Instant Pot. Add 1 cup water and half of the butter. Season with salt and pepper.
2. Put the steamer rack inside the pot, over the potatoes.
3. Sprinkle both sides of salmon with salt and pepper.
4. Seal the pot and set it to manual. Cook at high pressure for 3 minutes.
5. Transfer the salmon to a plate. Remove the potatoes and slice each in half.
6. Add the remaining butter to the pot. Add the garlic and cook until fragrant.
7. Put the potatoes back to the pot. Sprinkle with basil leaves and cook for 1 minute.
8. Serve salmon with potatoes.

Serving Suggestion: Garnish with lemon zest.

Tip: You can also add chopped parsley to the potatoes.

Nutritional Values Per Serving

Calories	Protein	Cholesterol	Total Fat	Saturated Fat
408	37.8 g	109 mg	22.6 g	8.9 g

Total Carbohydrate	Dietary Fiber	Total Sugars	Potassium	Sodium
15.1 g	2.9 g	0 g	1168 g	172 mg

CHAPTER 10: DINNER

Chicken Cheese Fillet

Servings: 4

Preparation Time: 15 minutes

Cooking Time: 25 minutes

Ingredients:

o 2 large chicken fillets

o 4 Gouda cheese slices

o 4 ham slices

o salt and pepper to taste

o 1 tbsp of chives, chopped

Directions:

1. Preheat your air fryer to 180° F.

2. Cut chicken fillet into four pieces. Make a slit horizontally to the edge.

3. Open the fillet and season with salt and pepper.

4. Cover each piece with chives and cheese slice.

5. Close fillet and wrap in a ham slice.

6. Place wrap chicken fillet into air fryer basket and cook for 15 minutes. Serve hot!

Nutritional Values Per Serving

Calories	Protein	Fat	Carbs
386	30 g	21 g	14.3 g

Servings: 4

Preparation Time: 10 minutes

Cooking Time: 30 minutes

Ingredients:

- 1 lettuce cut into broad strips
- 1 red bell pepper
- 1 tbsp of lemon juice
- 3 tbsp of rocket leaves
- black pepper to taste
- 2 tbsp of olive oil
- 3 tbsp of plain yogurt

Directions:

1. Preheat your air fryer to 200° F.
2. Place the bell pepper in air fryer basket and roast for 10 minutes.
3. Add pepper to a bowl, cover with a lid and set aside for 10 minutes.
4. Cut bell pepper into four parts and remove the seeds and skin.
5. Chop the bell pepper into strips.
6. Add lemon juice, yogurt, and oil in a bowl. Season with black pepper.
7. Add lettuce and rocket leaves and toss.
8. Garnish the salad with red bell pepper strips. Serve and enjoy!

Nutritional Values Per Serving

Calories	Protein	Fat	Carbs
91	2 g	7 g	3 g

Servings: 3

Preparation Time: 10 minutes

Cooking Time: 30 minutes

Ingredients

o   1 large whole wheat tortilla

o   ¼ cup of tomato pizza sauce

o   ¼ cup of pineapple tidbits

o   ¼ cup of mozzarella cheese, grated

o   ¼ cup of ham slice

Directions:

1.   Preheat your air fryer to 300° F.

2.   Place the tortilla on a baking sheet then spread pizza sauce over tortilla.

3.   Arrange ham slice, cheese, pineapple over the tortilla.

4.   Place the pizza in the air fryer basket and cook for 10 minutes. Serve hot.

Nutritional Values Per Serving

Calories	Protein	Fat	Carbs
80	4 g	2 g	12 g

Air Fryer Tortilla Pizza

Ingredients:

- 1 large whole wheat tortilla
- 1 tbsp of black olives
- salt and pepper to taste
- 4 tbsp of tomato sauce
- 8 pepperoni slices
- 3 tbsp of sweet corn
- 1 medium, tomato, chopped
- ½ cup of mozzarella cheese, grated

Directions:

1. Preheat your air fryer to 325° F.
2. Spread tomato sauce over tortilla.
3. Add pepperoni slices, olives, corn, tomato, and cheese on top of the tortilla.
4. Season with salt and pepper.
5. Place pizza in air fryer basket and cook for 7 minutes. Serve and enjoy!

Nutritional Values Per Serving

Calories	Protein	Fat	Carbs
110	4 g	5 g	10 g

Stuffed Garlic Chicken

Servings: 2

Preparation Time: 15 minutes

Cooking Time: 30 minutes

Ingredients:

o   ¼ cup of tomatoes, sliced

o   ½ tbsp of garlic, minced

o   2 basil leaves

o   salsa for serving

o   1 prosciutto slice

o   2 tsp of parmesan cheese, freshly grated

o   2 boneless chicken breasts

o   pepper and salt to taste

Directions:

1. Cut the side of the chicken breast to make a pocket.
2. Stuff each pocket with tomato slices, garlic, grated cheese and basil leaves.
3. Cut a slice of prosciutto in half to form 2 equal size pieces.
4. Season chicken with salt and pepper and wrap each with a slice of prosciutto.
5. Preheat your air fryer to 325° F.
6. Place the stuffed chicken breasts into air fryer basket and cook for 15 minutes.
7. Serve chicken breasts with salsa.

Nutritional Values Per Serving

Calories	Protein	Fat	Carbs	Dietary Fiber	Total Sugars
882	62 g	40 g	65 g	1 g	3 g

Rosemary Citrus Chicken

Servings: 2

Preparation Time: 15 minutes

Cooking Time: 30 minutes

Ingredients:

- 1 lb of chicken thighs
- ½ tsp of rosemary, fresh, chopped
- ⅛ tsp of thyme, dried
- ½ cup of tangerine juice
- 2 tbsp of white wine
- 1 tsp of garlic, minced
- salt and pepper to taste
- 2 tbsp of lemon juice

Directions:

1. Place the chicken thighs in a mixing bowl.
2. In another bowl, mix tangerine juice, garlic, white wine, lemon juice, rosemary, pepper, salt, and thyme.
3. Pour the mixture over chicken thighs and place in the fridge for 20 minutes.
4. Preheat your air fryer to 350° F and place your marinated chicken in air fryer basket and cook for 15 minutes. Serve hot and enjoy!

Nutritional Values Per Serving

Calories	Protein	Fat	Carbs
473	66 g	17 g	7 g

Servings: 2

Preparation Time: 15 minutes

Cooking Time: 30 minutes

Ingredients:

o 1 egg, beaten

o 4 tbsp of cheddar cheese, grated

o salt and pepper to taste

o ½ cup of macaroni and cheese

o 4 bread slices

Directions:

1. Spread the cheese and macaroni and cheese over the two bread slices.

2. Place the other bread slices on top of cheese and cut diagonally.

3. In a bowl, beat egg and season with salt and pepper.

4. Brush the egg mixture onto the bread.

5. Place the bread into air fryer and cook at 300° F for 5 minutes.

Nutritional Values Per Serving

Calories	Protein	Fat	Carbs
250	14 g	16 g	9 g

Cheese Burger Patties

Servings: 6

Preparation Time: 15 minutes

Cooking Time: 30 minutes

Ingredients:

o 1 lb of ground beef

o 6 cheddar cheese slices

o pepper and salt to taste

Directions:

1. Preheat your air fryer to 390° F.

2. Season beef with salt and pepper.

3. Make six round shaped patties from the mixture and place them into air fryer basket.

4. Air fry the patties for 10 minutes.

5. Open the air fryer basket and place cheese slices on top of patties and place into air fryer with an additional cook time of 1 minute.

Nutritional Values Per Serving

Calories	Protein	Fat	Carbs
253	29 g	14 g	0.4 g

Grilled Cheese Corn

Servings: 6

Preparation Time: 15 minutes

Cooking Time: 30 minutes

Ingredients:

o   2 whole corn on the cob, peel husks and discard silk

o   1 tsp of olive oil

o   2 tsp of paprika

o   ½ cup of feta cheese, grated

Directions:

1. Rub the olive oil over corn then sprinkle with paprika and rub all over the corn.

2. Preheat your air fryer to 300° F.

3. Place the seasoned corn on the grill for 15 minutes.

4. Place corn on a serving dish then sprinkle with grated cheese over corn.

Nutritional Values Per Serving

Calories	Protein	Fat	Carbs
150	7 g	10 g	7 g

Eggplant Fries

Servings: 4

Preparation Time: 20 minutes

Cooking Time: 30 minutes

Ingredients:

o   1 eggplant, cut into 3 inch pieces

o   ¼ cup of water

o   1 tbsp of olive oil

o   4 tbsp of cornstarch

o   sea salt to taste

Directions:

1.   Preheat your air fryer to 390° F.

2.   In a bowl, combine eggplant, water, oil, and cornstarch.

3.   Place the eggplant fries in air fryer basket, and air fry them for 20 minutes.

4.   Serve warm and enjoy!

Nutritional Values Per Serving

Calories	Protein	Cholesterol	Total Fat	Saturated Fat
135	9 g	68 mg	5 g	2 g

Total Carbohydrate	Dietary Fiber	Total Sugars	Sodium
15 g	4 g	6 g	577 mg

Servings: 2

Preparation Time: 5 minutes

Cooking Time: 30 minutes

Ingredients:

o   ½ cup of coconut oil, melted
o   zest of one lime
o   2 1 lb of grass fed skirt steaks
o   ¾ tsp of sea salt
o   1 tsp of red pepper flakes
o   1 tsp of ginger, fresh, grated
o   1 tbsp of garlic, minced
o   2 tbsp of freshly squeezed lime juice

Directions:

1. In a mixing bowl, combine lime juice, coconut oil, garlic, ginger, red pepper, salt, and zest.
2. Add the steaks and toss and rub with marinade.
3. Allow the meat to marinate for about 20 minutes at room temperature.
4. Transfer steaks to your air fryer directly on the rack.
5. Cook steaks in air fryer at 400° F for 5 minutes.

Nutritional Values Per Serving

Calories	Protein	Fat	Carbs
312	42.1 g	12.3 g	6.4 g

CHAPTER 11:

SNACK AND APPETIZERS

Servings: 4

Preparation Time: 10 minutes

Cooking Time: 15 minutes

Ingredients:

- o 1 pound of beef meat, ground
- o ¼ cup of panko breadcrumbs
- o a pinch of salt and black pepper
- o 3 tbsp of red onion, grated
- o ¼ cup of parsley, chopped
- o 2 garlic cloves, minced
- o 2 tbsp of lemon juice
- o zest of 1 lemon, grated
- o 1 egg
- o ½ tsp of cumin, ground
- o ½ tsp of coriander, ground
- o ¼ tsp of cinnamon powder
- o 2 oz of feta cheese, crumbled

Directions:

1. In a bowl, mix the beef with the breadcrumbs,
2. salt, pepper and the rest of the ingredients
3. except the cooking spray, stir well and shape medium balls out of this mix.
4. Arrange the meatballs on a baking sheet lined with parchment paper, grease them with cooking spray and bake at 450°F for 15 minutes.
5. Arrange the meatballs on a platter and serve as an appetizer.

Nutritional Values Per Serving

Calories	Protein	Fat	Carbs
300	35 g	6.4 g	22.4 g

Yogurt Dip

Servings: 6

Preparation Time: 10 minutes

Ingredients:

o   2 cups of Greek yogurt

o   2 tbsp of pistachios, toasted and chopped

o   a pinch of salt and white pepper

o   2 tbsp of mint, chopped

o   1 tbsp of kalamata olives, pitted and chopped

o   ¼ cup of za'atar spice

o   ¼ cup of pomegranate seeds

o   ⅓ cup of olive oil

Directions:

1.   In a bowl, combine the yogurt with the pistachios and the rest of the ingredients, whisk well, divide into small cups and serve with pita chips on the side.

Nutritional Values Per Serving

Calories	Protein	Fat	Carbs	Dietary Fiber
294	10 g	18 g	24 g	1 g

Tomato Bruschetta

Servings: 6

Preparation Time: 10 minutes

Cooking Time: 10 minutes

Ingredients:

o 1 baguette, sliced

o ⅓ cup of basil, chopped

o 6 tomatoes, cubed

o 2 garlic cloves, minced

o S pinch of salt and black pepper

o 1 tsp of olive oil

o 1 tbsp of balsamic vinegar

o ½ tsp of garlic powder

o cooking spray

Directions:

1. Arrange the baguette slices on a baking sheet lined with parchment paper, grease them with cooking spray and bake at 400° F for 10 minutes.

2. In a bowl, mix the tomatoes with the basil and the remaining ingredients, toss well and leave aside for 10 minutes.

3. Divide the tomato mix on each baguette slice, arrange them all on a platter and serve.

Nutritional Values Per Serving

Calories	Protein	Fat	Carbs	Dietary Fiber
162	4 g	4 g	29 g	7 g

Servings: 4

Preparation Time: 10 minutes

Cooking Time: 15 minutes

Ingredients:

- 5 tbsp of olive oil
- 2 garlic cloves, minced
- 2 tbsp of parsley, chopped
- 2 round whole wheat flatbreads
- 4 tbsp of parmesan, grated
- ½ cup of mozzarella cheese, grated
- 14 oz of canned artichokes, drained and quartered
- 1 cup of baby spinach, chopped
- ½ cup of cherry tomatoes, halved
- ½ tsp of basil, dried
- salt and black pepper to taste

Directions:

1. In a bowl, mix the parsley with the garlic and 4 tablespoons oil, whisk well and spread this over the flatbreads.
2. Sprinkle the mozzarella and half of the parmesan.
3. In a bowl, mix the artichokes with the spinach, tomatoes, basil, salt, pepper and the rest of the oil, toss and divide over the flatbreads as well.
4. Sprinkle the rest of the parmesan on top, arrange the flatbreads on a baking sheet lined with parchment paper and bake at 425° F for 15 minutes.

Nutritional Values Per Serving

Calories	Protein	Fat	Carbs	Dietary Fiber
223	7.4 g	11.2 g	15.5 g	5.34 g

Servings: 4

Preparation Time: 10 minutes

Ingredients:

o 7 oz of roasted red peppers, chopped

o ½ cup of parmesan, grated

o ⅓ cup of parsley, chopped

o 14 oz of canned artichokes, drained and chopped

o 3 tbsp of olive oil

o ¼ cup of capers, drained

o 1 and ½ tbsp of lemon juice

o 2 garlic cloves, minced

Directions:

1. In your blender, combine the red peppers with the parmesan and the rest of the ingredients and pulse well.

2. Divide into cups and serve as a snack.

Nutritional Values Per Serving

Calories	Protein	Fat	Carbs	Dietary Fiber
200	4.6 g	5.6 g	12.4 g	4.5 g

Coriander Falafel

Servings: 8

Preparation Time: 10 minutes

Cooking Time: 10 minutes

Ingredients:

- 1 cup of canned garbanzo beans, drained and rinsed
- 1 bunch of parsley leaves
- 1 yellow onion, chopped
- 5 garlic cloves, minced
- 1 tsp of coriander, ground
- a pinch of salt and black pepper
- ¼ tsp of cayenne pepper
- ¼ tsp of baking soda
- ¼ tsp of cumin powder
- 1 tsp of lemon juice
- 3 tbsp of tapioca flour
- olive oil for frying

Directions:

1. In your food processor, combine the beans with the parsley, onion and the rest the ingredients except the oil and the flour and pulse well.
2. Transfer the mix to a bowl, add the flour, stir well, shape 16 balls out of this mix and flatten them a bit.
3. Heat up a pan with some oil over medium-high heat, add the falafels, cook them for 5 minutes on each side, transfer to paper towels, drain excess grease, arrange them on a platter and serve as an appetizer.

Nutritional Values Per Serving

Calories	Protein	Fat	Carbs	Dietary Fiber
112	3.1 g	6.2 g	12.3 g	2 g

Red Pepper Hummus

Servings: 6

Preparation Time: 10 minutes

Ingredients:

o 6 oz of roasted red peppers, peeled and chopped
o 16 oz of canned chickpeas, drained and rinsed
o ¼ cup of Greek yogurt
o 3 tbsp of tahini paste
o juice of 1 lemon
o 3 garlic cloves, minced
o 1 tbsp of olive oil
o a pinch of salt and black pepper
o 1 tbsp of parsley, chopped

Directions:

1. In your food processor, combine the red peppers with the rest of the ingredients except the oil and the parsley and pulse well.
2. Add the oil, pulse again, divide into cups, sprinkle the parsley on top and serve as a party spread.

Nutritional Values Per Serving

Calories	Protein	Fat	Carbs	Dietary Fiber
255	6.5 g	11.4 g	17.4 g	4.5 g

White Bean Dip

Ingredients:

- 15 oz of canned white beans, drained and rinsed
- 6 oz of canned artichoke hearts, drained and quartered
- 4 garlic cloves, minced
- 1 tbsp of basil, chopped
- 2 tbsp of olive oil
- juice of ½ lemon
- zest of ½ lemon, grated
- salt and black pepper to taste

Directions:

1. In your food processor, combine the beans with the artichokes and the rest of the ingredients except the oil and pulse well.
2. Add the oil gradually, pulse the mix again, divide into cups and serve as a party dip.

Nutritional Values Per Serving

Calories	Protein	Fat	Carbs	Dietary Fiber
274	16.5 g	11.7 g	18.5 g	6.5 g

Hummus with Ground Lamb

Servings: 8

Preparation Time: 10 minutes

Cooking Time: 15 minutes

Ingredients:

o   10 oz of hummus

o   12 oz of lamb meat, ground

o   ½ cup of pomegranate seeds

o   ¼ cup of parsley, chopped

o   1 tbsp of olive oil

o   pita chips for serving

Directions:

1. Heat up a pan with the oil over medium-high heat, add the meat, and brown for 15 minutes stirring often.

2. Spread the hummus on a platter, spread the ground lamb all over, also spread the pomegranate seeds and the parsley and serve with pita chips as a snack.

Nutritional Values Per Serving

Calories	Protein	Fat	Carbs	Dietary Fiber
133	5 g	9.7 g	6.4 g	1.7 g

Eggplant Dip

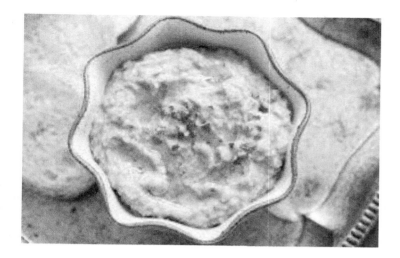

Servings: 4

Preparation Time: 10 minutes

Cooking Time: 40 minutes

Ingredients:

- 1 eggplant, poked with a fork
- 2 tbsp of tahini paste
- 2 tbsp of lemon juice
- 2 garlic cloves, minced
- 1 tbsp of olive oil
- salt and black pepper to taste
- 1 tbsp of parsley, chopped

Directions:

1. Put the eggplant in a roasting pan, bake at 400° F for 40 minutes, cool down, peel and transfer to your food processor.
2. Add the rest of the ingredients except the parsley, pulse well, divide into small bowls and serve as an appetizer with the parsley sprinkled on top.

Nutritional Values Per Serving

Calories	Protein	Fat	Carbs	Dietary Fiber
121	4.3 g	4.3 g	1.4 g	1 g

Veggie Fritters

Servings: 8

Preparation Time: 10 minutes

Cooking Time: 10 minutes

Ingredients:

- 2 garlic cloves, minced
- 2 yellow onions, chopped
- 4 scallions, chopped
- 2 carrots, grated
- 2 tsp of cumin, ground
- ½ tsp of turmeric powder
- salt and black pepper to taste
- ¼ tsp of coriander, ground
- 2 tbsp of parsley, chopped
- ¼ tsp of lemon juice
- ½ cup of almond flour
- 2 beets, peeled and grated
- 2 eggs, whisked
- ¼ cup of tapioca flour
- 3 tbsp of olive oil

Directions:

1. In a bowl, combine the garlic with the onions, scallions and the rest of the ingredients except the oil, stir well and shape medium fritters out of this mix.
2. Heat up a pan with the oil over medium-high heat, add the fritters, cook for 5 minutes on each side, arrange on a platter and serve.

Nutritional Values Per Serving

Calories	Protein	Fat	Carbs	Dietary Fiber
209	4.8 g	11.2 g	4.4 g	3 g

Bulgur Lamb Meatballs

Servings: 6

Preparation Time: 10 minutes

Cooking Time: 15 minutes

Ingredients:

- 1 and ½ cups of Greek yogurt
- ½ tsp of cumin, ground
- 1 cup of cucumber, shredded
- ½ tsp of garlic, minced
- a pinch of salt and black pepper
- 1 cup of bulgur
- 2 cups of water
- 1 pound of lamb, ground
- ¼ cup of parsley, chopped
- ¼ cup of shallots, chopped
- ½ tsp of allspice, ground
- ½ tsp of cinnamon powder
- 1 tbsp of olive oil

Directions:

1. In a bowl, combine the bulgur with the water, cover the bowl, leave aside for 10 minutes, drain and transfer to a bowl.
2. Add the meat, the yogurt and the rest of the ingredients except the oil, stir well and shape medium meatballs out of this mix.
3. Heat up a pan with the oil over medium-high heat, add the meatballs, cook them for 7 minutes on each side, arrange them all on a platter and serve as an appetizer.

Nutritional Values Per Serving

Calories	Protein	Fat	Carbs	Dietary Fiber
300	6.6 g	9.6 g	22.6 g	4.6 g

Cucumber Bites

Servings: 12

Preparation Time: 10 minutes

Ingredients:

o   1 English cucumber, sliced into 32 rounds

o   10 oz of hummus

o   16 cherry tomatoes, halved

o   1 tbsp of parsley, chopped

o   1 oz of feta cheese, crumbled

Directions:

1.   Spread the hummus on each cucumber round, divide the tomato halves on each, sprinkle the cheese and parsley on to and serve as an appetizer.

Nutritional Values Per Serving

Calories	Protein	Fat	Carbs	Dietary Fiber
162	2.4 g	3.4 g	6.4 g	2 g

Stuffed Avocado

Servings: 2

Preparation Time: 10 minutes

Ingredients:

- 1 avocado, halved and pitted
- 10 oz of canned tuna, drained
- 2 tbsp of sun-dried tomatoes, chopped
- 1 and ½ tbsp of basil pesto
- 2 tbsp of black olives, pitted and chopped
- salt and black pepper to taste
- 2 tsp of pine nuts, toasted and chopped
- 1 tbsp of basil, chopped

Directions:

1. In a bowl, combine the tuna with the sun-dried tomatoes and the rest of the ingredients except the avocado and stir.
2. Stuff the avocado halves with the tuna mix and serve as an appetizer.

Nutritional Values Per Serving

Calories	Protein	Fat	Carbs	Dietary Fiber
233	5.6 g	9 g	11.4 g	3.5 g

Wrapped Plums

Servings: 8

Preparation Time: 5 minutes

Ingredients:

o   2 oz of prosciutto, cut into 16 pieces

o   4 plums, quartered

o   1 tbsp of chives, chopped

o   a pinch of red pepper flakes, crushed

Directions:

1. Wrap each plum quarter in a prosciutto slice, arrange them all on a platter, sprinkle the chives and pepper flakes all over and serve.

Nutritional Values Per Serving

Calories	Protein	Fat	Carbs	Dietary Fiber
30	2 g	1 g	4 g	0 g

Cucumber Sandwich Bites

Servings: 12

Preparation Time: 5 minutes

Ingredients:

o   1 cucumber, sliced

o   8 slices of whole wheat bread

o   2 tbsp of cream cheese, soft

o   1 tbsp of chives, chopped

o   ¼ cup of avocado, peeled, pitted and mashed

o   1 tsp of mustard

o   salt and black pepper to taste

Directions:

1. Spread the mashed avocado on each bread slice, also spread the rest of the ingredients except the cucumber slices.

2. Divide the cucumber slices on the bread slices, cut each slice in thirds, arrange on a platter and serve as an appetizer.

Nutritional Values Per Serving

Calories	Protein	Fat	Carbs	Dietary Fiber
187	8.2 g	12.4 g	4.5 g	2.1 g

Cucumber Rolls

Servings: 6

Preparation Time: 5 minutes

Ingredients:

o   1 big cucumber, sliced lengthwise

o   1 tbsp of parsley, chopped

o   8 oz of canned tuna, drained and mashed

o   salt and black pepper to taste

o   1 tsp of lime juice

Directions:

1.   Arrange cucumber slices on a working surface, divide the rest of the ingredients, and roll.

2.   Arrange all the rolls on a platter and serve as an appetizer.

Nutritional Values Per Serving

Calories	Protein	Fat	Carbs	Dietary Fiber
200	3.5 g	6 g	7.6 g	3.4 g

Olives and Cheese Stuffed Tomatoes

Servings: 24

Preparation Time: 10 minutes

Ingredients:

- 24 cherry tomatoes, top cut off and insides scooped out
- 2 tbsp of olive oil
- ¼ tsp of red pepper flakes
- ½ cup pf feta cheese, crumbled
- 2 tbsp of black olive paste
- ¼ cup of mint, torn

Directions:

1. In a bowl, mix the olives paste with the rest of the ingredients except the cherry tomatoes and whisk well.
2. Stuff the cherry tomatoes with this mix, arrange them all on a platter and serve as an appetizer.

Nutritional Values Per Serving

Calories	Protein	Fat	Carbs	Dietary Fiber
136	5.1 g	8.6 g	5.6 g	4.8 g

Tomato Salsa

Servings: 6

Preparation Time: 5 minutes

Ingredients:

- o 1 garlic clove, minced
- o 4 tbsp of olive oil
- o 5 tomatoes, cubed
- o 1 tbsp of balsamic vinegar
- o ¼ cup of basil, chopped
- o 1 tbsp of parsley, chopped
- o 1 tbsp of chives, chopped
- o salt and black pepper to taste
- o pita chips for serving

Directions:

1. In a bowl, mix the tomatoes with the garlic and the rest of the ingredients except the pita chips, stir, divide into small cups and serve with the pita chips on the side.

Nutritional Values Per Serving

Calories	Protein	Fat	Carbs	Dietary Fiber
160	2.2 g	13.7 g	10.1 g	5.5 g

❖ Chili Mango and Watermelon Salsa

Servings: 12

Preparation Time: 5 minutes

Ingredients:

- 1 red tomato, chopped
- salt and black pepper to taste
- 1 cup of watermelon, seedless, peeled and cubed
- 1 red onion, chopped
- 2 mangos, peeled and chopped
- 2 chili peppers, chopped
- ¼ cup of cilantro, chopped
- 3 tbsp of lime juice
- pita chips for serving

Directions:

1. In a bowl, mix the tomato with the watermelon, the onion and the rest of the ingredients except the pita chips and toss well. Divide the mix into small cups and serve with pita chips on the side.

Nutritional Values Per Serving

Calories	Protein	Fat	Carbs	Dietary Fiber
62	2.3 g	4.7 g	3.9 g	1.3 g

Creamy Spinach and Shallots Dip

Servings: 4

Preparation Time: 10 minutes

Ingredients:

- 1 pound spinach, roughly chopped
- 2 shallots, chopped
- 2 tbsp of mint, chopped
- ¾ cup of cream cheese, soft
- salt and black pepper to taste

Directions:

1. In a blender, combine the spinach with the shallots and the rest of the ingredients, and pulse well. Divide into small bowls and serve as a party dip.

Nutritional Values Per Serving

Calories	Protein	Fat	Carbs	Dietary Fiber
204	5.9 g	11.5 g	4.2 g	3.1 g

Ingredients:

○ 8 oz of artichoke hearts, drained and quartered

○ ¾ cup of basil, chopped

○ ¾ cup of green olives, pitted and chopped

○ 1 cup of parmesan cheese, grated

○ 5 oz of feta cheese, crumbled

Directions:

1. In your food processor, mix the artichokes with the basil and the rest of the ingredients, pulse well, and transfer to a baking dish.
2. Introduce it in the oven, bake at 375° F for 30 minutes and serve as a party dip.

Nutritional Values Per Serving

Calories	Protein	Fat	Carbs	Dietary Fiber
186	1.5 g	12.4 g	2.6 g	0.9 g

Avocado Dip

Servings: 8

Preparation Time: 5 minutes

Ingredients:

- ½ cup of heavy cream
- 1 green chili pepper, chopped
- salt and pepper to taste
- 4 avocados, pitted, peeled and chopped
- 1 cup of cilantro, chopped
- ¼ cup of lime juice

Directions:

1. In a blender, combine the cream with the avocados and the rest of the ingredients and pulse well.
2. Divide the mix into bowls and serve cold as a party dip.

Nutritional Values Per Serving

Calories	Protein	Fat	Carbs	Dietary Fiber
200	7.6 g	14.5 g	8.1 g	3.8 g

Goat Cheese and Chives Spread

Ingredients:

- 2 oz of goat cheese, crumbled
- ¾ cup of sour cream
- 2 tbsp of chives, chopped
- 1 tbsp of lemon juice
- salt and black pepper to taste
- 2 tbsp of extra virgin olive oil

Directions:

1. In a bowl, mix the goat cheese with the cream and the rest of the ingredients and whisk really well.
2. Keep in the fridge for 10 minutes and serve as a party spread.

Nutritional Values Per Serving

Calories	Protein	Fat	Carbs	Dietary Fiber
220	5.6 g	11.5 g	8.9 g	4.8 g

Ginger and Cream Cheese Dip

Servings: 6

Preparation Time: 5 minutes

Ingredients:

- ½ cup of ginger, grated
- 2 bunches of cilantro, chopped
- 3 tbsp of balsamic vinegar
- ½ cup of olive oil
- 1 and ½ cups of cream cheese, soft

Directions:

1. In your blender, mix the ginger with the rest of the ingredients and pulse well.
2. Divide into small bowls and serve as a party dip.

Nutritional Values Per Serving

Calories	Protein	Fat	Carbs	Dietary Fiber
213	17.8 g	4.9 g	8.8 g	4.1 g

Walnuts Yogurt Dip

Ingredients:

- 3 garlic cloves, minced
- 2 cups of Greek yogurt
- ¼ cup of dill, chopped
- 1 tbsp of chives, chopped
- ¼ cup of walnuts, chopped
- salt and black pepper to taste

Directions:

1. In a bowl, mix the garlic with the yogurt and the rest of the ingredients, whisk well, divide into small cups and serve as a party dip.

Nutritional Values Per Serving

Calories	Protein	Fat	Carbs	Dietary Fiber
200	8.4 g	6.5 g	15.5 g	4.6 g

Herbed Goat Cheese Dip

Ingredients:

- ¼ cup of mixed parsley, chopped
- ¼ cup of chives, chopped
- 8 oz of goat cheese, soft
- salt and black pepper to taste
- a drizzle of olive oil

Directions:

1. In your food processor mix the goat cheese with the parsley and the rest of the ingredients and pulse well.

2. Divide into small bowls and serve as a party dip.

Nutritional Values Per Serving

Calories	Protein	Fat	Carbs	Dietary Fiber
245	11.2 g	11.3 g	8.9 g	4.5 g

◆ Scallions Dip ◆

Servings: 8

Preparation Time: 5 minutes

Ingredients:

- o 6 scallions, chopped
- o 1 garlic clove, minced
- o 3 tbsp of olive oil
- o salt and black pepper to taste
- o 1 tbsp of lemon juice
- o 1 and ½ cups cream cheese, soft
- o 2 oz of prosciutto, cooked and crumbled

Directions:

1. In a bowl, mix the scallions with the garlic and the rest of the ingredients except the prosciutto and whisk well.

2. Divide into bowls, sprinkle the prosciutto on top and serve as a party dip.

Nutritional Values Per Serving

Calories	Protein	Fat	Carbs	Dietary Fiber
144	5.5 g	7.7 g	6.3 g	1.4 g

← Tomato Cream Cheese Spread →

Servings: 6

Preparation Time: 5 minutes

Ingredients:

- 12 oz of cream cheese, soft
- 1 big tomato, cubed
- ¼ cup of homemade mayonnaise
- 2 garlic clove, minced
- 2 tbsp of red onion, chopped
- 2 tbsp of lime juice
- salt and black pepper to taste

Directions:

1. In your blender, mix the cream cheese with the tomato and the rest of the ingredients, pulse well, divide into small cups and serve cold.

Nutritional Values Per Serving

Calories	Protein	Fat	Carbs	Dietary Fiber
204	4.5 g	6.7 g	7.3 g	1.4 g

Pesto Dip

Ingredients:

- 1 cup of cream cheese, soft
- 3 tbsp of basil pesto
- salt and black pepper to taste
- 1 cup of heavy cream
- 1 tbsp of chives, chopped

Directions:

1. In a bowl, mix the cream cheese with the pesto and the rest of the ingredients and whisk well. Divide into small cups and serve as a party dip.

Nutritional Values Per Serving

Calories	Protein	Fat	Carbs	Dietary Fiber
230	5.4 g	14.5 g	6.5 g	4.8 g

Vinegar Beet Bites

Servings: 4

Preparation Time: 10 minutes

Cooking Time: 30 minutes

Ingredients:

- 2 beets, sliced
- a pinch of sea salt and black pepper
- ⅓ cup of balsamic vinegar
- 1 cup of olive oil

Directions:

1. Spread the beet slices on a baking sheet lined with parchment paper, add the rest of the ingredients, toss and bake at 350° F for 30 minutes.
2. Serve the beet bites cold as a snack.

Nutritional Values Per Serving

Calories	Protein	Fat	Carbs	Dietary Fiber
199	3.5 g	5.4 g	8.5 g	3.5 g

Zucchini and Olives Salsa

Servings: 4

Preparation Time: 5 minutes

Ingredients:

- ½ cup of black olives, pitted and sliced
- 3 zucchinis, cut with a spiralizer
- 1 cup of cherry tomatoes, halved
- salt and black pepper to taste
- 1 small red onion, chopped
- ½ cup of feta cheese, crumbled
- ½ cup of olive oil
- ¼ cup of apple cider vinegar

Directions:

1. In a bowl, mix the olives with the zucchinis and the rest of the ingredients, toss, divide into small cups and serve as an appetizer.

Nutritional Values Per Serving

Calories	Protein	Fat	Carbs	Dietary Fiber
140	1.4 g	14.2 g	3.5 g	1.4 g

Strawberry and Carrots Salad

Servings: 4

Preparation Time: 5 minutes

Ingredients:

- 6 carrots, peeled and grated
- 10 strawberries, halved
- salt and black pepper to taste
- 2 tbsp of balsamic vinegar
- 1 tbsp of Dijon mustard
- ¼ cup of lemon juice
- 2 tbsp of olive oil

Directions:

1. In a bowl, mix the carrots with the strawberries and the rest of the ingredients, toss, divide between appetizer plates and serve.

Nutritional Values Per Serving

Calories	Protein	Fat	Carbs	Dietary Fiber
182	3 g	4.3 g	7.5 g	2.4 g

Hot Squash Wedges

Servings: 6

Preparation Time: 10 minutes

Cooking Time: 25 minutes

Ingredients:

- 6 tbsp of olive oil
- 2 tbsp of chili paste
- 3 butternut squash, peeled and cut into wedges
- 2 tbsp of balsamic vinegar
- 1 tbsp of chives, chopped

Directions:

1. In a bowl, mix the squash wedges with the chili paste and the rest of the ingredients, toss, spread them on a baking sheet lined with parchment paper and bake at 400° F for 25 minutes, flipping them from time to time.
2. Divide the wedges into bowls and serve as a snack.

Nutritional Values Per Serving

Calories	Protein	Fat	Carbs	Dietary Fiber
180	1.4 g	4.2 g	6.5 g	4.4 g

Shrimp and Cucumber Bites

Servings: 8

Preparation Time: 5 minutes

Ingredients:

- 1 big cucumber, cubed
- 1 pound of shrimp, cooked, peeled, deveined and chopped
- 2 tbsp of heavy cream
- salt and black pepper to taste
- 12 whole grain crackers

Directions:

1. In a bowl, mix the cucumber with the rest of the ingredients except the crackers and stir well.
2. Arrange the crackers on a platter, spread the shrimp mix on each and serve.

Nutritional Values Per Serving

Calories	Protein	Fat	Carbs	Dietary Fiber
155	17.7 g	8.5 g	11.8 g	4.8 g

Servings: 12

Preparation Time: 5 minutes

Ingredients:

- o 1 big long cucumber, thinly sliced lengthwise
- o 2 tsp of lime juice
- o 4 oz of cream cheese, soft
- o 1 tsp of lemon zest, grated
- o salt and black pepper to taste
- o 2 tsp of dill, chopped
- o 4 oz of smoked salmon, cut into strips

Directions:

1. Arrange cucumber slices on a working surface and top each with a salmon strip.
2. In a bowl, mix the rest of the ingredients, stir and spread over the salmon.
3. Roll the salmon and cucumber strips, arrange them on a platter and serve as an appetizer.

Nutritional Values Per Serving

Calories	Protein	Fat	Carbs	Dietary Fiber
245	17.3 g	15.5 g	16.8 g	4.8 g

Eggplant Bombs

Servings: 6

Preparation Time: 10 minutes

Cooking Time: 45 minutes

Ingredients:

- 4 cups of eggplants, chopped
- 3 tbsp of olive oil
- 3 garlic cloves, minced
- 2 eggs, whisked
- salt and black pepper to taste
- 1 cup of parsley, chopped
- ½ cup of parmesan cheese, finely grated
- ¾ cups bread crumbs

Directions:

1. Heat up a pan with the oil over medium high heat, add the garlic and the eggplants, and cook for 15 minutes stirring often.
2. In a bowl, combine the eggplant mix with the rest of the ingredients, stir well and shape medium balls out of this mix.
3. Arrange the balls on a baking sheet lined with parchment paper and bake at 350° F for 30 minutes.

Nutritional Values Per Serving

Calories	Protein	Fat	Carbs	Dietary Fiber
224	3.5 g	10.6 g	5.4 g	1.8 g

Eggplant Bites

Servings: 8

Preparation Time: 10 minutes

Cooking Time: 15 minutes

Ingredients:

o 2 eggplants, cut into 20 slices

o 2 tbsp of olive oil

o ½ cup of roasted peppers, chopped

o ½ cup of kalamata olives, pitted and chopped

o 1 tbsp of lime juice

o 1 tsp of red pepper flakes, crushed

o salt and black pepper to taste

o 2 tbsp of mint, chopped

Directions:

1. In a bowl, mix the roasted peppers with the olives, half of the oil and the rest of the ingredients except the eggplant slices and stir well.

2. Brush eggplant slices with the rest of the olive oil on both sides, place them on the preheated grill over medium high heat, cook for 7 minutes on each side and transfer them to a platter.

3. Top each eggplant slice with roasted peppers mix and serve.

Nutritional Values Per Serving

Calories	Protein	Fat	Carbs	Dietary Fiber
214	5.4 g	10.6 g	15.4 g	5.8 g

CHAPTER 12: DESSERTS

Cold Lemon Squares

Servings: 4

Preparation Time: 30 minutes

Ingredients:

- o   1 cup of avocado oil + a drizzle
- o   2 bananas, peeled and chopped
- o   1 tbsp of honey
- o   ¼ cup of lemon juice
- o   a pinch of lemon zest, grated

Directions:

1. In your food processor, mix the bananas with the rest of the ingredients, pulse well and spread on the bottom of a pan greased with a drizzle of oil.
2. Put in the fridge for 30 minutes, slice into squares and serve.

Nutritional Values Per Serving

Calories	Protein	Fat	Carbs	Dietary Fiber
136	1.1 g	11.2 g	7 g	0.2 g

Servings: 6

Preparation Time: 10 minutes

Cooking Time: 30 minutes

Ingredients:

- ¾ cup of stevia
- 6 cups of blackberries
- ¼ cup of apples, cored and cubed
- ¼ tsp of baking powder
- 1 tbsp of lime juice
- ½ cup of almond flour
- ½ cup of water
- 3 and ½ tbsp of avocado oil
- cooking spray

Directions:

1. In a bowl, mix the berries with half of the stevia and lemon juice, sprinkle some flour all over, whisk and pour into a baking dish greased with cooking spray.

2. In another bowl, mix flour with the rest of the sugar, baking powder, the water and the oil, and stir the whole thing with your hands.

3. Spread over the berries, introduce in the oven at 375° F and bake for 30 minutes. Serve warm.

Nutritional Values Per Serving

Calories	Protein	Fat	Carbs	Dietary Fiber
221	9 g	6.3 g	6 g	3.3 g

Black Tea Cake

Servings: 8

Preparation Time: 10 minutes

Cooking Time: 35 minutes

Ingredients:

o 6 tbsp of black tea powder

o 2 cups of almond milk, warmed up

o 1 cup of avocado oil

o 2 cups of stevia

o 4 eggs

o 2 tsp of vanilla extract

o 3 and ½ cups of almond flour

o 1 tsp of baking soda

o 3 tsp of baking powder

Directions:

1. In a bowl, combine the almond milk with the oil, stevia and the rest of the ingredients and whisk well.

2. Pour this into a cake pan lined with parchment paper, introduce in the oven at 350° F and bake for 35 minutes.

3. Leave the cake to cool down, slice and serve.

Nutritional Values Per Serving

Calories	Protein	Fat	Carbs	Dietary Fiber
200	5.4 g	6.4 g	6.5 g	4 g

Green Tea and Vanilla Cream

Servings: 4

Preparation Time: 2 hours

Ingredients:

- o 14 oz of almond milk, hot
- o 2 tbsp of green tea powder
- o 14 oz of heavy cream
- o 3 tbsp of stevia
- o 1 tsp of vanilla extract
- o 1 tsp of gelatin powder

Directions:

1. In a bowl, combine the almond milk with the green tea powder and the rest of the ingredients, whisk well, cool down, divide into cups and keep in the fridge for 2 hours before serving.

Nutritional Values Per Serving

Calories	Protein	Fat	Carbs	Dietary Fiber
120	4 g	3 g	7 g	3 g

Figs Pie

Servings: 8

Preparation Time: 10 minutes

Cooking Time: 1 hour

Ingredients:

- ½ cup of stevia
- 6 figs, cut into quarters
- ½ tsp of vanilla extract
- 1 cup of almond flour
- 4 eggs, whisked

Directions:

1. Spread the figs on the bottom of a spring form pan lined with parchment paper.
2. In a bowl, combine the other ingredients, whisk and pour over the figs,
3. Bake at 375° F for 1 hour, flip the pie upside down when it's done and serve.

Nutritional Values Per Serving

Calories	Protein	Fat	Carbs	Dietary Fiber
200	8 g	4.4 g	7.6 g	3 g

Cherry Cream

Servings: 4

Preparation Time: 2 hours

Ingredients:

- 2 cups of cherries, pitted and chopped
- 1 cup of almond milk
- ½ cup of whipping cream
- 3 eggs, whisked
- ⅓ cup of stevia
- 1 tsp of lemon juice
- ½ tsp of vanilla extract

Directions:

1. In your food processor, combine the cherries with the milk and the rest of the ingredients, pulse well, divide into cups and keep in the fridge for 2 hours before serving.

Nutritional Values Per Serving

Calories	Protein	Fat	Carbs	Dietary Fiber
200	3.4 g	4.5 g	5.6 g	3.3 g

Strawberries Cream

Servings: 4

Preparation Time: 10 minutes

Cooking Time: 20 minutes

Ingredients:

o   ½ cup of stevia

o   2 pounds of strawberries, chopped

o   1 cup of almond milk

o   zest of 1 lemon, grated

o   ½ cup of heavy cream

o   3 egg yolks, whisked

Directions:

1. Heat up a pan with the milk over medium-high heat, add the stevia and the rest of the ingredients, whisk well, simmer for 20 minutes, divide into cups and serve cold.

Nutritional Values Per Serving

Calories	Protein	Fat	Carbs	Dietary Fiber
152	0.8 g	4.4 g	5.1 g	5.5 g

Apples and Plum Cake

Servings: 4

Preparation Time: 10 minutes

Cooking Time: 40 minutes

Ingredients:

- 7 oz of almond flour
- 1 egg, whisked
- 5 tbsp of stevia
- 3 oz of warm almond milk
- 2 pounds of plums, pitted and cut into quarters
- 2 apples, cored and chopped
- zest of 1 lemon, grated
- 1 tsp of baking powder

Directions:

1. In a bowl, mix the almond milk with the egg, stevia, and the rest of the ingredients except the cooking spray and whisk well.
2. Grease a cake pan with the oil, pour the cake mix inside, introduce in the oven and bake at 350° F for 40 minutes.
3. Cool down, slice and serve.

Nutritional Values Per Serving

Calories	Protein	Fat	Carbs	Dietary Fiber
209	6.6 g	6.4 g	8 g	6 g

Cinnamon Chickpeas Cookies

Servings: 12

Preparation Time: 10 minutes

Cooking Time: 20 minutes

Ingredients:

o 1 cup of canned chickpeas, drained, rinsed and mashed

o 2 cups of almond flour

o 1 tsp of cinnamon powder

o 1 tsp of baking powder

o 1 cup of avocado oil

o ½ cup of stevia

o 1 egg, whisked

o 2 tsp of almond extract

o 1 cup of raisins

o 1 cup of coconut, unsweetened and shredded

Directions:

1. In a bowl, combine the chickpeas with the flour, cinnamon and the other ingredients, and whisk well until you obtain a dough.

2. Scoop tablespoons of dough on a baking sheet lined with parchment paper, introduce them in the oven at 350° F and bake for 20 minutes.

3. Leave them to cool down for a few minutes and serve.

Nutritional Values Per Serving

Calories	Protein	Fat	Carbs	Dietary Fiber
200	2.4 g	4.5 g	9.5 g	3.4 g

Cocoa Brownies

Servings: 8

Preparation Time: 10 minutes

Cooking Time: 20 minutes

Ingredients:

- 30 oz of canned lentils, rinsed and drained
- 1 tbsp of honey
- 1 banana, peeled and chopped
- ½ tsp of baking soda
- 4 tbsp of almond butter
- 2 tbsp of cocoa powder
- cooking spray

Directions:

1. In a food processor, combine the lentils with the honey and the other ingredients except the cooking spray and pulse well.
2. Pour this into a pan greased with cooking spray, spread evenly, introduce in the oven at 375° F and bake for 20 minutes.
3. Cut the brownies and serve cold.

Nutritional Values Per Serving

Calories	Protein	Fat	Carbs	Dietary Fiber
200	4.3 g	4.5 g	8.7 g	2.4 g

Cardamom Almond Cream

Servings: 4

Preparation Time: 30 minutes

Ingredients:

- juice of 1 lime
- ½ cup of stevia
- 1 and ½ cups of water
- 3 cups of almond milk
- ½ cup of honey
- 2 tsp of cardamom, ground
- 1 tsp of rose water
- 1 tsp of vanilla extract

Directions:

1. In a blender, combine the almond milk with the cardamom and the rest of the ingredients.
2. Pulse well, divide into cups and keep in the fridge for 30 minutes before serving.

Nutritional Values Per Serving

Calories	Protein	Fat	Carbs	Dietary Fiber
283	7.1 g	11.8 g	4.7 g	0.3 g

Banana Cinnamon Cupcakes

Servings: 4

Preparation Time: 10 minutes

Cooking Time: 20 minutes

Ingredients:

- 4 tbsp of avocado oil
- 4 eggs
- ½ cup of orange juice
- 2 tsp of cinnamon powder
- 1 tsp of vanilla extract
- 2 bananas, peeled and chopped
- ¾ cup of almond flour
- ½ tsp of baking powder
- cooking spray

Directions:

1. In a bowl, combine the oil with the eggs, orange juice and the other ingredients except the cooking spray.
2. Whisk well, pour in a cupcake pan greased with the cooking spray.
3. Introduce it in the oven at 350° F and bake for 20 minutes.
4. Cool the cupcakes down and serve.

Nutritional Values Per Serving

Calories	Protein	Fat	Carbs	Dietary Fiber
142	1.6 g	4.2 g	5.7 g	4.2 g

Rhubarb and Apples Cream

Servings: 6

Preparation Time: 10 minutes

Ingredients:

- o   3 cups of rhubarb, chopped
- o   1 and ½ cups of stevia
- o   2 eggs, whisked
- o   ½ tsp of nutmeg, ground
- o   1 tbsp of avocado oil
- o   ⅓ cup of almond milk

Directions:

1. In a blender, combine the rhubarb with the stevia and the rest of the ingredients.
2. Pulse well, divide into cups and serve cold.

Nutritional Values Per Serving

Calories	Protein	Fat	Carbs	Dietary Fiber
200	2.5 g	5.2 g	7.6 g	3.4 g

Almond Rice Dessert

Servings: 4

Preparation Time: 10 minutes

Cooking Time: 20 minutes

Ingredients:

- 1 cup of white rice
- 2 cups of almond milk
- 1 cup of almonds, chopped
- ½ cup of stevia
- 1 tbsp of cinnamon powder
- ½ cup of pomegranate seeds

Directions:

1. In a pot, mix the rice with the milk and stevia, bring to a simmer and cook for 20 minutes, stirring often.
2. Add the rest of the ingredients, stir, divide into bowls and serve.

Nutritional Values Per Serving

Calories	Protein	Fat	Carbs	Dietary Fiber
234	6.5 g	9.5 g	12.4 g	3.4 g

Peach Sorbet

Servings: 4

Preparation Time: 2 hours

Cooking Time: 10 minutes

Ingredients:

o   2 cups of apple juice

o   1 cup of stevia

o   2 tbsp of lemon zest, grated

o   2 pounds of peaches, pitted and quartered

Directions:

1. Heat up a pan over medium heat, add the apple juice and the rest of the ingredients, simmer for 10 minutes.

2. Transfer it to a blender and pulse.

3. Divide into cups and keep in the freezer for 2 hours before serving.

Nutritional Values Per Serving

Calories	Protein	Fat	Carbs	Dietary Fiber
182	5.4 g	5.4 g	12 g	3.4 g

Cranberries and Pears Pie

Servings: 4

Preparation Time: 10 minutes

Cooking Time: 40 minutes

Ingredients:

- 2 cups of cranberries
- 3 cups of pears, cubed
- a drizzle of olive oil
- 1 cup of stevia
- ⅓ cup of almond flour
- 1 cup of rolled oats
- ¼ avocado oil

Directions:

1. In a bowl, mix the cranberries with the pears and the other ingredients except the olive oil and the oats, and stir well.
2. Grease a cake pan with the a drizzle of olive oil, pour the pears mix inside, sprinkle the oats all over and bake at 350° F for 40 minutes.
3. Cool the mix down, and serve.

Nutritional Values Per Serving

Calories	Protein	Fat	Carbs	Dietary Fiber
172	4.5 g	3.4 g	11.5 g	4.3 g

Lemon Cream

Servings: 6

Preparation Time: 1 hour

Cooking Time: 10 minutes

Ingredients:

o   2 eggs, whisked

o   1 and ¼ cup of stevia

o   10 tbsp of avocado oil

o   1 cup of heavy cream

o   juice of 2 lemons

o   zest of 2 lemons, grated

Directions:

1.   In a pan, combine the cream with the lemon juice and the other ingredients.

2.   Whisk well and cook it for 10 minutes.

3.   Divide into cups and keep in the fridge for 1 hour before serving.

Nutritional Values Per Serving

Calories	Protein	Fat	Carbs	Dietary Fiber
200	4.5 g	8.5 g	8.6 g	4.5 g

Vanilla Cake

Servings: 10

Preparation Time: 10 minutes

Cooking Time: 25 minutes

Ingredients:

- 3 cups of almond flour
- 3 tsp of baking powder
- 1 cup of olive oil
- 1 and ½ cup of almond milk
- 1 and ⅔ cup of stevia
- 2 cups of water
- 1 tbsp of lime juice
- 2 tsp of vanilla extract
- cooking spray

Directions:

1. In a bowl, mix the almond flour with the baking powder, the oil and the rest of the ingredients except the cooking spray and whisk well.
2. Pour the mix into a cake pan greased with the cooking spray, introduce in the oven and bake at 370° F for 25 minutes.
3. Leave the cake to cool down, cut and serve!

Nutritional Values Per Serving

Calories	Protein	Fat	Carbs	Dietary Fiber
200	4.5 g	2.5 g	5.5 g	2.5 g

Servings: 2

Preparation Time: 5 minutes

Cooking Time: 5 minutes

Ingredients:

- o   2 cups of canned pumpkin flesh
- o   2 tbsp of stevia
- o   1 tsp of vanilla extract
- o   2 tbsp of water
- o   a pinch of pumpkin spice

Directions:

1. In a pan, combine the pumpkin flesh with the other ingredients and simmer it for 5 minutes.
2. Divide into cups and serve cold.

Nutritional Values Per Serving

Calories	Protein	Fat	Carbs	Dietary Fiber
192	3.5 g	3.4 g	7.6 g	4.5 g

Chia and Berries Smoothie Bowl

Servings: 2

Preparation Time: 5 minutes

Ingredients:

- 1 and ½ cup of almond milk
- 1 cup of blackberries
- ¼ cup of strawberries, chopped
- 1 and ½ tbsp of chia seeds
- 1 tsp of cinnamon powder

Directions:

1. In a blender, combine the blackberries with the strawberries and the rest of the ingredients, pulse well, divide into small bowls and serve cold.

Nutritional Values Per Serving

Calories	Protein	Fat	Carbs	Dietary Fiber
182	3 g	3.4 g	8 g	3.4 g

Minty Coconut Cream

Servings: 2

Preparation Time: 4 minutes

Ingredients:

o   1 banana, peeled

o   2 cups of coconut flesh, shredded

o   3 tbsp of mint, chopped

o   1 and ½ cups of coconut water

o   2 tbsp of stevia

o   ½ avocado, pitted and peeled

Directions:

1. In a blender, combine the coconut with the banana and the rest of the ingredients.

2. Pulse well, divide it into cups and serve cold.

Nutritional Values Per Serving

Calories	Protein	Fat	Carbs	Dietary Fiber
193	3 g	5.4 g	7.6 g	3.4 g

Watermelon Cream

Ingredients:

- 1 pound of watermelon, peeled and chopped
- 1 tsp of vanilla extract
- 1 cup of heavy cream
- 1 tsp of lime juice
- 2 tbsp of stevia

Directions:

1. In a blender, combine the watermelon with the cream and the rest of the ingredients.
2. Pulse well, divide it into cups and keep in the fridge for 15 minutes before serving.

Nutritional Values Per Serving

Calories	Protein	Fat	Carbs	Dietary Fiber
122	0.4 g	5.7 g	5.3 g	3.2 g

Servings: 4

Preparation Time: 10 minutes

Cooking Time: 10 minutes

Ingredients:

o ⅔ cup of stevia

o 1 tbsp of olive oil

o ⅓ cup of coconut water

o 1 tsp of vanilla extract

o 1 tsp of lemon zest, grated

o 2 cup of red grapes, halved

Directions:

1. Heat up a pan with the water over medium heat, add the oil, stevia and the rest of the ingredients.

2. Toss it, simmer for 10 minutes, divide into cups and serve.

Nutritional Values Per Serving

Calories	Protein	Fat	Carbs	Dietary Fiber
122	0.4 g	3.7 g	2.3 g	1.2 g

Servings: 4

Preparation Time: 2 hours

Ingredients:

- ½ cup of cocoa powder
- ¾ cup of red cherry jam
- ¼ cup of stevia
- 2 cups of water
- 1 pound of cherries, pitted and halved

Directions:

1. In a blender, mix the cherries with the water and the rest of the ingredient.
2. Pulse well, divide it into cups and keep in the fridge for 2 hours before serving.

Nutritional Values Per Serving

Calories	Protein	Fat	Carbs	Dietary Fiber
162	1 g	3.4 g	5 g	2.4 g

Apple Couscous Pudding

Servings: 4

Preparation Time: 10 minutes

Cooking Time: 25 minutes

Ingredients:

- ½ cup of couscous
- 1 and ½ cups of milk
- ¼ cup of apple, cored and chopped
- 3 tbsp of stevia
- ½ tsp of rose water
- 1 tbsp of orange zest, grated

Directions:

1. Heat up a pan with the milk over medium heat, add the couscous and the rest of the ingredients.
2. Whisk it, simmer for 25 minutes, divide into bowls and serve.

Nutritional Values Per Serving

Calories	Protein	Fat	Carbs	Dietary Fiber
150	4 g	4.5 g	7.5 g	5.5 g

Ricotta Ramekins

Servings: 4

Preparation Time: 10 minutes

Cooking Time: 1 hour

Ingredients:

- 6 eggs, whisked
- 1 and ½ pounds of ricotta cheese, soft
- ½ pound of stevia
- 1 tsp of vanilla extract
- ½ tsp of baking powder
- cooking spray

Directions:

1. In a bowl, mix the eggs with the ricotta and the other ingredients except the cooking spray and whisk well.
2. Grease 4 ramekins with the cooking spray, pour the ricotta cream in each and bake at 360° F for 1 hour.
3. Serve cold.

Nutritional Values Per Serving

Calories	Protein	Fat	Carbs	Dietary Fiber
180	4 g	5.3 g	11.5 g	5.4 g

Papaya Cream

Servings: 2

Preparation Time: 10 minutes

Ingredients:

- 1 cup of papaya, peeled and chopped
- 1 cup of heavy cream
- 1 tbsp of stevia
- ½ tsp of vanilla extract

Directions:

1. In a blender, combine the cream with the papaya and the other ingredients.
2. Pulse well, divide it into cups and serve cold.

Nutritional Values Per Serving

Calories	Protein	Fat	Carbs	Dietary Fiber
182	2 g	3.1 g	3.5 g	2.3 g

Almonds and Oats Pudding

Servings: 4

Preparation Time: 10 minutes

Cooking Time: 15 minutes

Ingredients:

- o   1 tbsp of lemon juice
- o   zest of 1 lime
- o   1 and ½ cups of almond milk
- o   1 tsp of almond extract
- o   ½ cup of oats
- o   2 tbsp of stevia
- o   ½ cup of silver almonds, chopped

Directions:

1. In a pan, combine the almond milk with the lime zest and the other ingredients, whisk, bring to a simmer and cook over medium heat for 15 minutes.
2. Divide the mix into bowls and serve cold.

Nutritional Values Per Serving

Calories	Protein	Fat	Carbs	Dietary Fiber
174	4.8 g	12.1 g	3.9 g	3.2 g

Chocolate Cups

Servings: 6

Preparation Time: 2 hours

Ingredients:

- ½ cup of avocado oil
- 1 cup of melted chocolate
- 1 tsp of matcha powder
- 3 tbsp of stevia

Directions:

1. In a bowl, mix the chocolate with the oil and the rest of the ingredients.
2. Whisk it really well, divide into cups and keep in the freezer for 2 hours before serving.

Nutritional Values Per Serving

Calories	Protein	Fat	Carbs	Dietary Fiber
174	2.8 g	9.1 g	3.9 g	2.2 g

Mango Bowls

Servings: 4

Preparation Time: 30 minutes

Ingredients:

- 3 cups of mango, cut into medium chunks
- ½ cup of coconut water
- ¼ cup of stevia
- 1 tsp of vanilla extract

Nutritional Values Per Serving

Calories	Protein	Fat	Carbs	Dietary Fiber
122	4.5 g	4 g	6.6 g	5.3 g

Cocoa and Pears Cream

Servings: 4

Preparation Time: 10 minutes

Ingredients:

o 2 cups of heavy creamy
o ⅓ cup of stevia
o ¾ cup of cocoa powder
o 6 oz of dark chocolate, chopped
o zest of 1 lemon
o 2 pears, chopped

Directions:

1. In a blender, combine the cream with the stevia and the rest of the ingredients.

2. Pulse well, divide it into cups and serve cold.

Nutritional Values Per Serving

Calories	Protein	Fat	Carbs	Dietary Fiber
172	4 g	5.6 g	7.6 g	3.5 g

Pineapple Pudding

Servings: 4

Preparation Time: 10 minutes

Cooking Time: 40 minutes

Ingredients:

o   3 cups of almond flour

o   ¼ cup of olive oil

o   1 tsp of vanilla extract

o   2 and ¼ of cups stevia

o   3 eggs, whisked

o   1 and ¼ cup of natural apple sauce

o   2 tsp of baking powder

o   1 and ¼ cups of almond milk

o   2 cups of pineapple, chopped

o   cooking spray

Directions:

1. In a bowl, combine the almond flour with the oil and the rest of the ingredients except the cooking spray and stir well.

2. Grease a cake pan with the cooking spray, pour the pudding mix inside, introduce in the oven and bake at 370° F for 40 minutes.

3. Serve the pudding cold.

Nutritional Values Per Serving

Calories	Protein	Fat	Carbs	Dietary Fiber
223	3.4 g	8.1 g	7.6 g	3.4 g

Lime Vanilla Fudge

Servings: 6

Preparation Time: 3 hours

Ingredients:

- ⅓ cup of cashew butter
- 5 tbsp of lime juice
- ½ tsp of lime zest, grated
- 1 tbsp of stevia

Directions:

1. In a bowl, mix the cashew butter with the other ingredients and whisk well.
2. Line a muffin tray with parchment paper, scoop 1 tablespoon of lime fudge mix in each of the muffin tins and keep in the freezer for 3 hours before serving.

Nutritional Values Per Serving

Calories	Protein	Fat	Carbs	Dietary Fiber
200	5 g	4.5 g	13.5 g	3.4 g

Mixed Berries Stew

Servings: 6

Preparation Time: 10 minutes

Cooking Time: 15 minutes

Ingredients:

o   zest of 1 lemon, grated

o   juice of 1 lemon

o   ½ pint of blueberries

o   1 pint of strawberries, halved

o   2 cups of water

o   2 tbsp of stevia

Directions:

1. In a pan, combine the berries with the water, stevia and the other ingredients.

2. Bring it to a simmer, cook over medium heat for 15 minutes, divide into bowls and serve cold.

Nutritional Values Per Serving

Calories	Protein	Fat	Carbs	Dietary Fiber
172	2.3 g	7 g	8 g	3.4 g

Orange and Apricots Cake

Servings: 8

Preparation Time: 10 minutes

Cooking Time: 20 minutes

Ingredients:

- ¾ cup of stevia
- 2 cups of almond flour
- ¼ cup of olive oil
- ½ cup of almond milk
- 1 tsp of baking powder
- 2 eggs
- ½ tsp of vanilla extract
- juice and zest of 2 oranges
- 2 cups of apricots, chopped

Directions:

1. In a bowl, mix the stevia with the flour and the rest of the ingredients, whisk and pour into a cake pan lined with parchment paper.
2. Introduce in the oven at 375° F, bake for 20 minutes, cool down, slice and serve.

Nutritional Values Per Serving

Calories	Protein	Fat	Carbs	Dietary Fiber
221	5 g	8.3 g	14.5 g	3.4 g

Blueberry Cake

Servings: 6

Preparation Time: 10 minutes

Cooking Time: 30 minutes

Ingredients:

- 2 cups of almond flour
- 3 cups of blueberries
- 1 cup of walnuts, chopped
- 3 tbsp of stevia
- 1 tsp of vanilla extract
- 2 eggs, whisked
- 2 tbsp of avocado oil
- 1 tsp of baking powder
- cooking spray

Directions:

1. In a bowl, combine the flour with the blueberries, walnuts and the other ingredients except the cooking spray, and stir well.
2. Grease a cake pan with the cooking spray, pour the cake mix inside, introduce everything in the oven at 350° F and bake for 30 minutes.
3. Cool the cake down, slice and serve.

Nutritional Values Per Serving

Calories	Protein	Fat	Carbs	Dietary Fiber
225	4.5 g	9 g	10.2 g	4.5 g

Blueberry Yogurt Mousse

Ingredients:

- ○ 2 cups of Greek yogurt
- ○ ¼ cup of stevia
- ○ ¾ cup of heavy cream
- ○ 2 cups of blueberries

Directions:

1. In a blender, combine the yogurt with the other ingredients.
2. Pulse well, divide it into cups and keep in the fridge for 30 minutes before serving.

Nutritional Values Per Serving

Calories	Protein	Fat	Carbs	Dietary Fiber
141	0.8 g	4.7 g	8.3 g	4.7 g

Chapter 13: 28 Day

Mediterranean Meal Plan

MAIN FOOD LIST

VEGETABLES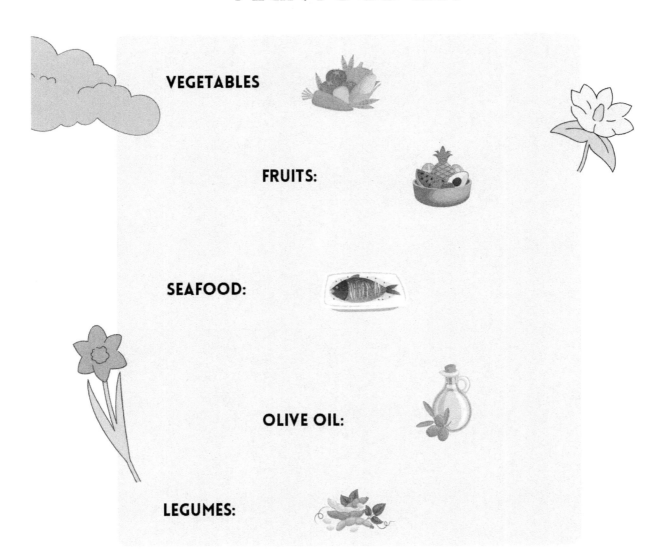

FRUITS:

SEAFOOD:

OLIVE OIL:

LEGUMES:

WEEK: ____1____

	BREAKFAST	LUNCH	DINNER	SNACKS
MON	Pineapple Green Smoothie 297kcal	Mediterranean Tuna Spinach Salad 375kcal	Dijon Salmon with Green Bean Pilaf 442kcal	Blackberries 46kcal
TUE	Banana overnight oats 377kcal	Stuffed sweet potatoes 387kcal	Quiches with smoked potatoes 238kcal	Cauliflower rice 119kcal
WED	Sweet potatoes 22kcal	Mediterranean chickpea salad 300kcal	Zucchini noodle caprese 300kcal	Green Goddess hummus 119kcal
THU	Shakshuka 146kcal	Lentil soup 421kcal	Garlic grilled shrimp skewers 190kcal	Roasted cauliflower hummus 235kcal
FRI	Kale & Butternut Squash Frittata 220kcal	Baked tuna meatballs 243kcal	Dijon baked salmon 249kcal	Salmon avocado salad 732kcal
SAT	Breakfast Egg Muffins 134kcal	Cucumber salad 45kcal	Zucchini pasta with shrimp 306kcal	Falafel 48kcal
SUN	Easy Oatmeal 260kcal	Beet soup 145kcal	Mediterranean Tilapia 197kcal	baba ganoush 86kcal

WEEK: _____2_____

	BREAKFAST	LUNCH	DINNER	SNACKS
MON	Potato Omelet 176kcal	Baked cod 258kcal	Pesto gnocchi 321kcal	Corn on the Cob 94kcal
TUE	Pumpkin Parfait 43kcal	Baked sweet potato 102kcal	Pasta Puttanesca 343kcal	Creamy Whipped Feta Dip 139kcal
WED	Poached Eggs 343kcal	Quinoa Tabbouleh 150kcal	Turkey Meatballs 252kcal	Cooked Basmati Rice 199kcal
THU	Vegetable Frittata 136kcal	Eggplant Caponata 147kcal	Shrimp Risotto 552kcal	Niçoise Salad 332kcal
FRI	Olive Oil Granola 392kcal	Creamy Mushroom Risotto 442kcal	Roasted squash 362kcal	Roasted Carrots 64kcal
SAT	Green Smoothie 92kcal	Pesto Salmon 272kcal	Mushroom Galette 188kcal	Avocado hummus 149kcal
SUN	Banana Bread 200kcal	Chickpea soup 240kcal	Eggplant Casserole 309kcal	Sweet Potato Stew 128kcal

WEEK: _____3_____

	BREAKFAST	LUNCH	DINNER	SNACKS
MON	Feta and Spinach Frittata 152kcal	Tortellini Salad 255kcal	Turmeric Lemon Chicken Soup 167kcal	Mediterranean watermelon salad 192kcal
TUE	Zucchini Quiche 145kcal	Stuffed Grape Leaves 25kcal	Za'atar Garlic Spinach Pasta 397kcal	Greek lemon rice 145kcal
WED	French Toast 452kcal	Olive Oil Fried Brussels Sprouts 285kcal	Salmon Burgers 137kcal	Salmon Cakes 350kcal
THU	Mediterranean Sandwiches 242kcal	Salmon Salad 474kcal	Spaghetti Aglio e Olio 399kcal	Wheat Berry Pudding 212kcal
FRI	Fig & Ricotta Overnight Oats 294kcal	Fish Piccata 357kcal	Garlic Mushroom Pasta 488kcal	Chocolate Chip Cookies 188kcal
SAT	Broccoli Frittata 255kcal	Fennel Orange Salad 63kcal	Mediterranean Bean Soup 366kcal	Tahini Date Banana Shake 299kcal
SUN	Caprese Avocado Toast 329kcal	Black Eyed Peas 46kcal	Roasted Carrot Soup 148kcal	Rice pudding 366kcal

WEEK: _____4_____

	BREAKFAST	LUNCH	DINNER	SNACKS
MON	Blueberry Smoothie 211kcal	Eggplant Lasagna 119kcal	Artichoke Garden Flatbread Pizza 145kcal	Mediterranean Bean Salad 211kcal
TUE	Acai bowl 141kcal	Seafood Paella 516kcal	Blackened Salmon 390kcal	Avocado Salsa 208kcal
WED	Pumpkin Waffles 447kcal	Eggplant Rollatini 193kcal	Roasted Cauliflower Soup 250kcal	Roasted Peppers 38kcal
THU	Zucchini Muffins 178kcal	Lemon Broccoli Pesto Pasta 555kcal	Harissa Lamb Chops 132kcal	Vegan Eggplant "Meatballs" 50kcal
FRI	Homemade Muesli 336kcal	Easy Meatball Soup 297kcal	Poached Halibut 341kcal	Pita Chips 14kcal
SAT	Peach Overnight Oats 369kcal	Roasted Cauliflower and Chickpea Stew 286kcal	Stuffed Zucchini 172kcal	Eggplant Caponata 91kcal
SUN	Berry Chia Pudding 343kcal	Pumpkin Soup 214kcal	Mediterranean Zucchini Boats 438kcal	fish sticks 119kcal

CONCLUSION

The Mediterranean diet is not a strict plan. Or maybe, it's a method for eating that emphasizes natural products, vegetables, whole grains, vegetables and olive oil. Fish is the principle protein source rather than red meat, pork or poultry. And indeed, it remembers red wine-for balance. Aged dairy are consumed normally but in moderate sums. Eggs and poultry are occasionally expended, but red meat and prepared foods are not eaten normally.

Finally, if You've found this book helpful in any way,

an Amazon review is always welcome!

Thank You!

Yours sincerely,

Susan Lombardi

Printed in Great Britain
by Amazon

82462404R00127